PARIS

a journey through time

LEONARD PITT

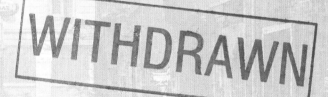
COUNTERPOINT

BERKELEY

Acknowledgements

Many people helped in the making of this book. Most notably, Alexandre
Gady, art historian and lecturer at the Sorbonne. His generosity in sharing his
vast knowledge of Paris through our many animated conversations was most
important. Francoise Reynaud and her colleagues at the Musée Carnavalet,
Catherine Tambrun and Jean-Baptiste Wolloch, were always gracious in
receiving me in their archives. Luc Passion at the Bibliotheque Historique de la
Ville de Paris had a wonderful knack for interceding when I needed him most.
Summer Allmann, an expert in Paris history, spent many hours walking Paris
streets with me helping to unravel the many mysteries of this great city. And
Donald Galfond, the indefatigable eagle-eye who pointed out inconsistencies
and errors in detail that are the bane of any writer.

❧

Library of Congress Cataloging-in-Publication Data

Pitt, Leonard, 1941–
Paris : a journey through time / by Leonard Pitt.
p. cm.
ISBN-13: 978-1-58243-622-7
ISBN-10: 1-58243-622-3
1. Paris (France)—Pictorial works. 2. Paris (France—Description and travel.
3. Social change—France—Paris—History—Pictorial works. 4. Documentary photography—France—Paris.
5. Paris (France)—Tours. 6. Walking—France—Paris—Guidebooks. 7. Paris (France)—Maps. I. Title.

DC707.P541 2010
914.4'36100222—dc22
2010022158

Cover design by Domini Dragoone
Printed in China

COUNTERPOINT
1919 Fifth Street
Berkeley, CA 94710

www.counterpointpress.com

Distributed by Publishers Group West

10 9 8 7 6 5 4 3 2 1

For my brother Barry

Contents

*An asterisk, in a title or in the text, designates a street that no longer exists.

▲ Rue Brisemiche in the old Saint-Merri quarter.

Introduction

During the forty-plus years I have been going to Paris, I have watched the city grow and change. I knew Les Halles when it was still a thriving food market intimately tied to the soul of Paris. I knew the city skyline before it was darkened by the shadow of a skyscraper. I knew what it was to walk Paris streets for miles and never see a parking meter because they did not yet exist. I knew the monuments of Paris, like Notre Dame and the Louvre, when they were black with soot and the Marais when it was still a shunned quarter before it transformed into a jewel of the city. But only after I began serious study of Paris history did I come to understand the many forces that have shaped the city.

Early on I learned that my initial assumptions about Paris were wrong. The Louvre, for example, did not spring out of a single architectural drawing but rather evolved over seven hundred years, transforming from a medieval fortress to a royal residence and finally to a world-class museum. Similarly, in the physical layout of Paris, I assumed that the city's design was the result of a reasoned process of deliberation taking into account issues of population growth, changing centers of industry and commerce, and so on. Only after much study did I learn how chance, fate, accident, greed, and the individual choices of ordinary citizens have played so great a role in shaping Paris.

Place des Vosges never would have seen the light of day were it not for the fatal injury suffered by Henri II when his opponent's lance pierced his eye during a jousting tournament held at the Hôtel des Tournelles in 1559. In her grief, the queen, Catherine de Medici, ordered the palace demolished, thus opening the space for the Place des Vosges. The ripple effect of this accident continued to shape Paris for centuries. Distraught, Catherine de Medici fled the Marais and moved to the Louvre. Had she not made this move, she would not have chosen to build the Palais des Tuileries, which means the Grand Galerie would not have been built to connect the two structures, which means the Louvre as we know it today would not exist, nor the Tuileries, nor the Place de la Concorde and the Champs Elysées.

On a more modest scale, the pages that follow show us how destiny has continued to play its hand in Paris, at times succeeding and at other times failing. Time alone tells us whether these transformations were inspired moments of urban planning or mediocre calculations in the service of misguided goals.

▲ Rue Galande seen from Place Maubert before demolition. (photo, Blancard)

Maubert and Saint-Séverin

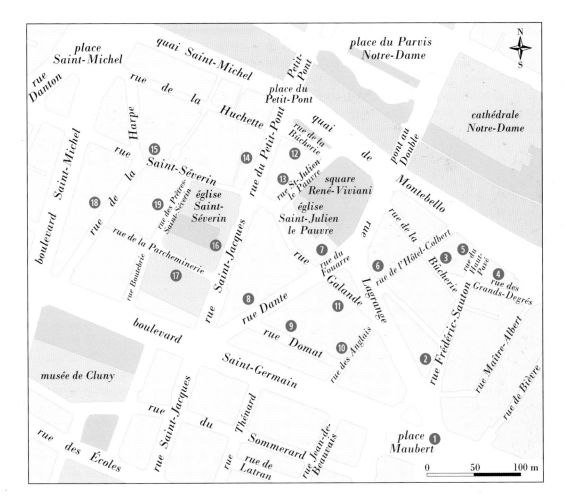

Place Maubert ❶

At its origins in the early 12th century, Place Maubert was a center of scholarship and learning in a growing university quarter that was full of schools, student hostels, inns, cafés, and restaurants. Because it was also a traffic hub connecting roads leading into and out of Paris, it was an important meeting and departure point for travelers. The *place* lost much of its animation in the mid-13th century, when the student population began moving up the hill to new colleges erected on Montagne Sainte-Geneviève.

By the early 16th century, under Francois I, the *place* took on the sinister character of a public execution site.

People sentenced to torture on the rack, to burning at the stake, or to hanging met a grisly end here, many of them Protestants during the wars of religion. Among them was erudite Etienne Dolet, strangled and burned on this spot in 1547 for printing tracts judged heretical by the Catholic Church. A bronze statue in his memory, erected here around 1887, was stolen and melted down by the Nazis during World War II. The base stood empty for decades until the present-day square with its fountain was installed in the 1980s.

The old Place Maubert stood about fifty yards to the north of today's *place* and was demolished in stages, first for the creation of Boulevard Saint-Germain (1855), and second for Rue Lagrange (1887). The only houses remaining of the old *place* are on the east of today's Place Maubert at the entrance to Rue Frédéric-Sauton.

During the 19th century and much of the 20th century, Place Maubert was described by writers as the "lower depths" of Paris, a debauched quarter of sordid hotels, cafés, and restaurants with a population of rag pickers, alcoholics, thieves, prostitutes, and pimps. As late as 1957 a headless body was found in a phone booth a few steps away at the corner of Rue de la Bûcherie and Rue Frédéric-Sauton. Walking through these streets today, with their trendy shops and restaurants, one would have little idea of the makeover this quarter has undergone in recent years.

▼ Map. Paris in the 18th century. In orange, Rue Galande, leading to Place Maubert and Rue Saint-Victor. In green, Couvent des Carmes (Carmelite convent). In blue, Rue des Noyers*, today's Boulevard Saint-Germain. In red, a fortification erected by Philippe Auguste, circa 1200. (Turgot map, 18th century)

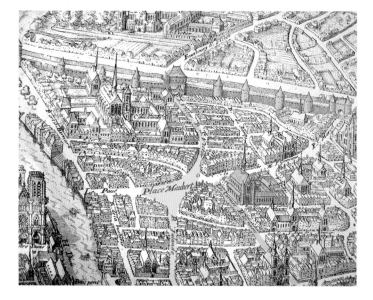

▲ Place Maubert towards Rue Frédéric-Sauton, circa 1865. In the distance, Notre Dame. (photo, Marville)

Haussmann's Project for the Extension of Place Maubert

Haussmann's approach to the remaking of Place Maubert was similar to his plan for extending Rue de Rennes to the Seine. In both cases a thoroughfare arrives at Boulevard Saint-Germain and then divides into three streets branching out to the river.

The idea behind this urban design was to facilitate traffic circulation and unify the city with a system of roadways that would link sections of the Left and Right Banks that were isolated from each other.

The map to the right shows Haussmann's plan for the Rennes extension and how drastically it would have affected not only the quarter of Saint-Germain-des-Prés but the river itself, with the loss of the Pont des Arts and the addition of two new bridges, one that would have disfigured the tip of Ile de la Cité.

The Monge extension across Boulevard Saint-Germain was only partially carried out with Rue Lagrange. Had that extension been completed according to Haussmann's plans, we would have lost Rue Frédéric-Sauton, Rue Maître-Albert, and Rue de Bièvre.

It is fortunate that the Rennes extension dragged on for so many years, into the 1940s, until the sensibility of the public had changed and the idea became untenable. Traffic today does not flow as easily as many might wish, but Paris has survived nevertheless and a historic quarter is intact, adding immeasurably to the richness of the city.

Photos of the quarter around the old Place Maubert before the opening of Rue Lagrange show what was lost for the creation of this street. (See page 14.) In all appearances, the long segment of Rue Galande that was torn down had all the character and feel of Rue Bonaparte with a slight curve to it. To be sure, the appeal of moving quickly through a dense urban fabric is most seductive, but when comparing old Rue Galande to Rue Lagrange, one wonders if the trade was worth it.

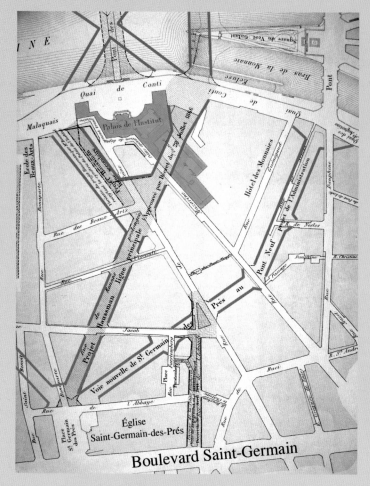

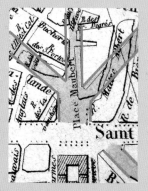

▲ Paris Administration's plan for the Rue de Rennes extension to the Seine, 1866. Note the elimination of the Pont des Arts at the top, to be replaced with an X-shaped bridge, and an additional bridge crossing the tip of Ile de la Cité. Note how the new street cuts through the 17th-century Institut de France in green. The eastern part of the quarter is eviscerated by a street leading from Place Saint-Germain-des-Prés to Pont Neuf.

◄ Place Maubert with Haussmann's proposed new streets. Note the similarity to the Rue de Rennes extension. Rue Monge crosses Boulevard Saint-Germain and splits in three. On the right, a proposed street that would have obliterated Rue Maître-Albert and Rue de Bièvre. In the middle, a proposed widening of Rue Frédéric-Sauton. On the left, Rue Lagrange. Of the three, only the latter was carried out. (map, Andriveau Goujon, 1863)

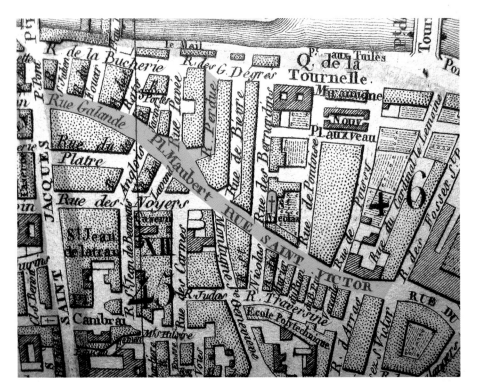

▲ Before the creation of Rue des Ecoles, Rue Monge, and Boulevard Saint-Germain, Place Maubert was part of a continuous thoroughfare comprised of Rue Galande and Rue Saint-Victor. In blue, Rue Maître-Albert. In red, the Church of Saint-Nicolas-du-Chardonnet. (map, Hérisson, 1822)

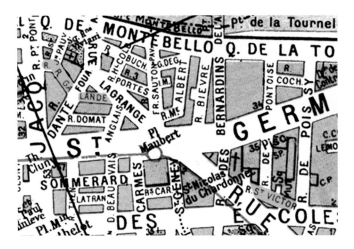

► In green, remnants of Rue Galande (left) and Rue Saint-Victor (right) after the opening of Rue Lagrange, Rue Monge, Rue des Ecoles, and Boulevard Saint-Germain.

▲ Rue Galande from Place Maubert. Everything here will be torn down for Rue Lagrange. On the left, Rue des Lavandières*. The facade on the right, with blue windows, is 2 Rue Galande; 4 Rue Galande has pink windows. Compare to the next page. The red line is over 1 Rue Galande and matches the red line in the photo below. (photo, Blancard)

◀ Rue des Lavandières*. The cross street is Rue Galande. The building on the right with a red line above the wording is 1 Rue Galande. This street leads to Rue des Noyers*, today's Boulevard Saint-Germain. (photo, Marville)

▲ Rue Frédéric-Sauton, viewed from Place Maubert. All buildings to the left of the red line will be demolished for the creation of Rue Lagrange. (photo, Blancard)

▶ Neighborhoods of Maubert and Saint-Séverin. In yellow, new streets proposed by Haussmann. Only three projects were carried out: the widening of Rue Saint-Jacques (1), and the creation of Rues Lagrange (2) and Dante (3). Three others never got off the drawing board: the widening of Rue Frédéric-Sauton (4), a street running alongside the Church of Saint-Julien le Pauvre, in blue (5), and a street cutting through Rue Maître-Albert (6). (map, Andriveau Goujon, 1863)

▲ Demolition of Rue Galande in preparation for Rue Lagrange, March 9, 1889. On the left, a 17th-century stairway at 11 Rue Galande is exposed. The building colored blue is 2 Rue Galande, and the one colored red is 4 Rue Galande. Compare to pp. 14, 15. Note the new Haussmann building on the left with balconies and compare with the photo below; it's the same building. (photo, Emonts; ©Musée Carnavalet/Roger-Viollet)

▶ Same view today. The building on the left is the same as in the photo above.

▲ Building undergoing demolition. This 17th-century staircase with balustrade, at 11 Rue Galande, is visible in the photo above.

▲ Demolition for Rue Lagrange is complete and reveals buildings on Rue des Trois-Portes. On the left, a statue of Etienne Dolet, burned at the stake on this spot along with his heretical books in 1546. The statue was melted down by the Germans during the Occupation. In the distance, Notre Dame. (photo, Godefroy)

► Same view today. On the left, Rue Lagrange. To the right of the Haussmann buildings, we see the entry into Rue des Trois-Portes off Rue Frédéric-Sauton.

▲ Place Maubert looking south, circa 1887. Sidewalks are under construction for the new opening of Rue Frédéric-Sauton. Compare the wrought-iron balcony on the left to the same in the photo below. Behind the statue of Etienne Dolet is the Marché des Carmes, which was torn down in 1934. (photo, Godefroy)

◀ Same view today.

Rue Frédéric-Sauton ❷

Rue Frédéric-Sauton evolved as an extension of Place Maubert. Long before Quai de Montebello was constructed, the street ended in a stone stairway that led down to the Seine. Several of the houses on the east side of the street, on the right in these photos, have the curious feature of cellars that connect with buildings on the neighboring Rue Maître-Albert. Number 19 is particularly curious. The cellar contains a number of small vaulted cells, each with a small narrow opening leading to the next. This cellar leads to a stairway that in turn leads to a trapdoor that opens onto 16 Rue Maître-Albert. Had Haussmann's plans been fully carried out, all the buildings in this street would have been lost in a massive project of street widening.

▼ Rue Frédéric-Sauton, circa 1910. (photo, Atget)

◀ Same view today.

Rue de la Bûcherie ❸

▲ Rue de la Bûcherie, view west, circa 1940.

◀ Same view today. In the 1960s, a hotel room on this street cost one dollar a night.

Rue des Grands-Degrés ❹

▶ Rue des Grands-Degrés from Rue de la Bûcherie. On the left, Rue du Haut-Pavé. On the right, Rue Frédéric-Sauton. Compare building on the left with the red line to the photo on the next page. (photo, Marville)

▼ Same view today.

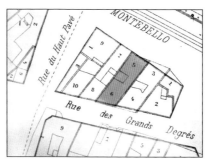

◀ This map shows the absurdity of the 1849 law regarding alignment. The building in red stretching from the quai to Rue des Grands-Degrés extended beyond the alignment by a mere 1.6 inches and was to have the facades on both ends torn off and rebuilt in order to conform to the required alignment.

Rue du Haut-Pavé ⑤

▲ Corner of Rue de la Bûcherie (left) and Rue du Haut-Pavé, from the 1940s. Compare the building with the red line to the old photograph on the previous page. That building was demolished in the 1950s. In the distance, Notre Dame.

◄ Same view today.

Rues Lagrange and de l'Hôtel-Colbert ⑥

Rue Lagrange was created in 1887 as an extension of Rue Monge. It was to connect with the Right Bank via a street running in front of Notre Dame as part of Haussmann's plan to unify the different quarters of the city by a network of efficient thoroughfares.

The opening of Rue Lagrange brought about the destruction of a network of medieval streets in this quarter. Rue des Anglais, for centuries a lively street, was cut in half and today stands inert. Much of Rue Galande and most of Rue du Fouarre were also lost.

Rue de l'Hôtel-Colbert was opened in 1202 through a vineyard, the Clos Mauvoisin, and for over 400 years was known as Rue des Rats. It was granted a name change in 1829 at the request of the street's inhabitants. Lost to demolition was 20 Rue de l'Hôtel-Colbert, an impressive mansion with remarkable bas-reliefs in the courtyard. See next page.

▲ Rue de l'Hôtel-Colbert towards Rue Galande from Rue des Trois-Portes. The arch on the right is the entry to the mansion Hôtel Colbert at number 20. (photo, Godefroy)

◀ Same view today. In the foreground, Rue Lagrange. The buildings facing you are on Rue Galande. Compare the arched doorway in the middle of the photo to the same at the end of the street in the photo above.

▲ Courtyard to Hôtel Colbert at 20 Rue de l'Hôtel-Colbert. Demolished in 1887 for the creation of Rue Lagrange.

▲ Rue de l'Hôtel-Colbert from Rue Galande towards Quai de Montebello. Everything to the left of the red line, plus everything on the right side of the street, was demolished for Rue Lagrange. See this street from the opposite direction on p. 23. (photo, Marville)

► Same view today. Note the red line.

Rue du Fouarre ❼

With only three buildings remaining on one side of the street, one could walk by Rue du Fouarre and never know it was there. The rest of the street was demolished for the creation of Rue Lagrange. The street was opened in 1202 through the vineyard Clos Mauvoisin and originally ran from Rue Galande to Rue de la Bûcherie. With the founding of the University in the 13th century, a number of colleges were established here, making this street an early center of university activity.

Originally known as Rue des Ecoliers, the street took on its present name in the 14th century. Fouarre derives from *feurre*, old French for "straw," because students were made to sit on straw during their outdoor lessons as a sign of abnegation before their teachers. Dante Alighieri was a student here in 1304, hence the adjacent Rue Dante. At night a chain was drawn across both ends of the street in an attempt to control the rowdy antics of students. The opening of Rue Lagrange in 1887 all but eliminated the street.

▲ Rue du Fouarre looking towards the Seine, 1865. Notice the low wall at the end of the street. Compare to pp. 27 and 28. Everything here was demolished for Rue Lagrange. In the distance is Notre Dame. (photo, Marville)

◀ In blue, the Church of Saint-Julien le Pauvre. In green, Rue Galande. In orange, Rue du Fouarre. Note the number of schools along the latter: Ecole à la Nation d'Angleterre, Ecole à la Nation de Picardie, Grand Ecole de Normandie, Grand Ecole de France, Petite Ecole de France.

▲ Rue du Fouarre from Quai de Montebello, 1865. The house at the end of the street is on Rue Galande. The building on the right with a green line at the very top is the annex to the hospital, Hôtel Dieu. Compare to pp. 28 and 31. The blue line on the left also matches pp. 30 and 31. In the foreground is Rue de la Bûcherie. With the exception of three buildings, down the street on the right, everything here was demolished for Rue Lagrange. (photo, Marville)

▲ Red, Rue du Fouarre before the creation of Rue Lagrange, seen here outlined in blue.

◄ Point of view from arrow in map above.

▲ Rue du Fouarre seen from Quai de Montebello. This photo was taken several years later. Demolition for Rue Lagrange has begun. In the foreground is Rue de la Bûcherie. The building with the green line is the Hôtel Dieu annex. Compare to p. 27. Notice the addition of the sign on the building advertising an *imprimerie* (print shop), absent on the previous page. (photo, Godefroy)

▲ Rue Lagrange, 1899. Under the arrow is 49 Rue Galande, demolished when Rue Dante was cut through. Compare to p. 27. Note the sign "Imprimerie," and compare to previous page; this building no longer stands. The Hôtel Dieu annex, denoted by the green line on p. 28, has been torn down. The building with the red line still stands. (photo, Atget)

▼ Same view today. Note that Rue Dante has been cut through. Compare the red line to the same in the photo above.

▼ A section of Rue Galande demolished for Rue Dante. The arrow points to number 49. Compare to top photo and to p. 27.

▲ On the left, Notre Dame. On the right is the chapel to the Hôtel Dieu. The building with the red line is the annex to Hôtel Dieu on the Left Bank. Compare the blue line in the middle of the photo to the photo below. (photo, Richebourg)

◄ Compare blue line to the same in the photo above. Note that the arch has been squared. The building on the right stands in place of the Hôtel Dieu annex that was torn down for the opening of Rue Lagrange in the 1880s. (photo, Brichaud, 1899)

▲ View from the towers of Notre Dame, circa 1900. The red line shows the layout of the old Rue du Fouarre. In blue, the section of Rue de la Bûcherie eliminated to create Square René Viviani. The building on the right with a green line is the Hôtel Dieu annex, originally shortened for Rue Lagrange and later demolished. Compare the building on the left with a blue line over the door to the photos on the previous page.

▶ Rue de la Bûcherie seen from Rue Lagrange. In blue, on the right, is the Prefecture de Police on Ile de la Cité. It is the only thing standing today. Everything else has been torn down. The stretch of Rue de la Bûcherie pictured here is highlighted in blue in the photo above. The building on the left with a green line is the same as in the photo above and on pp. 27 and 28. The second-story walkway links two wings of the Hôtel Dieux annex and crosses over Rue de la Bûcherie. This section of the street was eliminated in 1908 for Square René Viviani.

▲ Rue Lagrange looking north. The building on the left with a green line is the annex of the Hôtel Dieu on the Quai de Montebello in the process of being shortened. Compare to the bottom photo on the previous page. The building with the blue line is Haussmann's newly built Hôtel Dieu. (photo, Godefroy, circa 1887)

◄ Same view today.

▲ View looking south of Rue Lagrange in construction. The row of buildings in the distance is on Rue Galande, and the arrow indicates 29 Rue Galande before the roof was squared off. Compare to the building in the middle in the photo on the right. (photo, Godefroy, circa 1887)

▼ Same view today. The row of buildings above stands behind the more modern buildings in the distance.

▲ Actual view of 29 Rue Galande (in the center), without its gable.

Rue
Dante ⑧

Rue Dante was part of Haussmann's network of new thoroughfares to facilitate movement through Paris. The street was created in stages from 1855 to 1897. An excavation found evidence of a Jewish cemetery dating back to the late 12th century. At the intersection of Rue Dante, Boulevard Saint-Germain, and Rue Saint-Jacques stood a chapel completed in 1357, founded in the name of Saint Yves, patron saint of lawyers. The chapel was closed during the Revolution and torn down in 1793.

▲ Demolition in preparation for the construction of Rue Dante. The corner building with a red line is on Rue Galande and dates to the 17th century. It matches the white building on the left in the photo below. (photo, Atget, 1900)

◀ A closer view of Rue Dante leading to Rues du Fouarre and Lagrange. On the left, Rue Galande. The white building on the left has a red line in the photo above.

▲ Rue Dante empty of vehicles not long after completion. The first street on the right, Rue Domat, was formerly Rue du Plâtre.

▶ Same view today.

◀ In color: houses to be expropriated for the second phase of Rue Dante.

Rue Domat 9

▼ Buildings in Rue Domat under demolition, 1900. Match red line to photo above. (photo, Atget)

▲ Same view today. The building on the right is the same in both photos.

Rue des Anglais ⑩

Rue des Anglais was created in the early 13th century as a link between Rue Galande and Rue des Noyers*. Its inert state today gives no clue to the great animation this street once knew. Its name derives from the English students who lodged here in the Middle Ages and attended classes in nearby Rue du Fouarre or Place Maubert.

During the Revolution a notorious nightspot, Cabaret du Père Lunette, opened here at number 4. It became famous as part of the Lower Depths of Paris, a night haunt frequented by pimps, prostitutes, thieves, and counterfeiters. An underground passageway leading to the sewers gave quick egress to those in too much of a hurry to use the front door.

▲ Rue des Anglais, looking towards Rue Galande. The first left is Rue du Plâtre, today's Rue Domat. (photo, Marville)

◄ Same view today.

Rue Galande ⑪

Rue Galande is one of the oldest streets in Paris, dating back to Roman times. It led to Lyon and Rome through a connection to Rue de la Montagne Sainte-Geneviève. In 1202 the street took on the name Rue Garlande because it passed through vineyards owned by Mathilde Garlande. Rue Galande was actually widened to its present width of eight meters (8.75 yards) in 1672, which gives us insight into how a cultural sense of space changes through time. Imagine how narrow it must have been before.

In the 17th century, it was considered one of the most beautiful streets in Paris. By 1900, as the city grew and economic and commercial patterns changed, Rue Galande became one of the darker corners of Paris, visited by tourists seeking local color. Through the 1960s, hotels here were still barely two dollars a night. Like the rest of the quarter, it has gone seriously upscale in recent years.

▼ Same view today.

▲ A remnant of Rue Galande between Rue Dante and Rue Lagrange that survived the creation of Rue Lagrange visible in the distance. (photo, Atget, 1899)

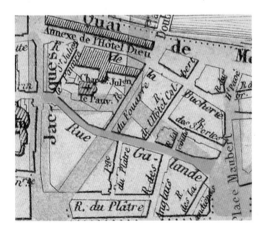

◄ In blue, Rue Galande in its entirety from Rue Saint-Jacques to Place Maubert.

▲In blue, remnants of Rue Galande after the creation of Rues Dante and Lagrange.

◄ Rue Galande, circa 1860. The building on the left corner was torn down to widen Rue Saint-Julien le Pauvre around 1908. (photo, Marville)

▲ In red, the proposed street that would have amputated Rue Galande, in blue, to facilitate traffic from Rue Saint-Jacques to Rue Lagrange. This would have put the church of Saint-Julien le Pauvre, today pleasantly secluded, onto a busy street. (map, Andriveau Goujon, 1863)

▲ Corner of Rue Galande and Rue Saint-Julien le Pauvre after demolition of the corner building, 1940s.

▲ Same view today.

Rue de la Bûcherie ⑫

Rue de la Bûcherie was opened in 1202 through the vineyard Clos Mauvoisin and connected Place Maubert to today's Rue du Petit-Pont, at that time the site of a fortress known as Petit Châtelet. The name derives from a port (Port aux Bûches) that existed at this point on the Seine, where for over three hundred years the enormous quantities of wood used in Paris were delivered. In the 16th century, the port moved to Ile des Louviers on the Right Bank.

In the 14th century, medical instruction became independent of the church and was made one of the faculties of the university. After years of moving around Paris, the faculty was established here in 1469–1470. The amphitheater pictured below was constructed in 1773–1775. The site fell into private hands in 1816 and passed through a number of commercial uses (e.g., a laundry, café, boarding house, brothel). It was bought by the city in 1896 and restored in 1909–1912.

▲ ◀ Faculty of Medicine before and after restoration in 1909–1912. Today the building houses administrative offices for the Préfecture de la Seine. (photo above, Atget, 1902)

◄ Faculty of Medicine undergoing restoration, 1909–1912. (photo, Barry, 1909)

▼ Same view today.

◄▼ Rue de la Bûcherie looking east. The photo on the left dates from 1899, and the photo below from circa 1910. Two wings of the annex to the Hôtel Dieu are connected by a walkway. The annex was demolished in 1908. This section of the street was obliterated for Square René Viviani. Compare to p. 31. (photo, Atget)

▲ Same view today. Compare the building on the right to the building in blue in the photo below.

425. PARIS – Ancien Hôtel-Dieu pris de la Rue de la Bucherie
J. H.

◀ Rue de la Bûcherie from Rue du Petit-Pont shortly after the annex to Hôtel Dieu had been cleared.

▼ On the left, Rue de la Bûcherie, eliminated in 1928 when this space, now empty of the Hôtel Dieu annex, became Square René Viviani. Other proposals were put forth for this space: One was to build apartments, and a second to build a museum to Christian civilization. (photo, Pottier, 1909)

Rue Saint-Julien le Pauvre

▼ View from today's Square René Viviani before it became a garden. On the right is Rue Saint-Julien le Pauvre. The building with the green line still stands and is visible in the present-day photo. The arched entry leads to Hôtel Laffemas at 14 Rue Saint-Julien le Pauvre. (photo, Atget)

► Same view today.

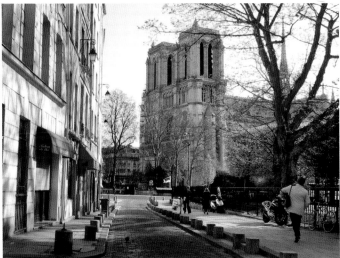

▲ Rue Saint-Julien le Pauvre. The cross street is Rue de la Bûcherie. The large building straight ahead is the Hôtel Dieu annex on Quai de Montebello that was demolished in 1908. (photo, Atget, 1902)

◀ Same view today.

Rue du Petit-Pont ⑭

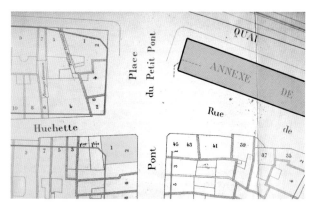

▲ This map shows the extent of reconfiguring intended for this intersection. The widening of Rue de la Huchette according to this plan would have called for the demolition of all the buildings on that street. The blue area is the Hôtel de Bourgogne, shown in the photo on the next page. The Hôtel Dieu annex is highlighted in green.

◄ A view of Rue du Petit-Pont north towards the Seine, before widening. On the left, Rue Saint-Séverin. On the right, Rue Galande. All the buildings on the left side were torn down for street widening in 1908. The corner building with a blue line is the same as the one on p. 50, but is viewed from a different angle. The building on the right corner was torn down later, not for widening but for a more modern construction.

▲ Place du Petit-Pont leading to Rue du Petit-Pont. On the extreme left is the Hôtel Dieu annex. The row of buildings colored blue was torn down for the widening of Rue du Petit-Pont in 1908. Compare to the buildings on the left in the photo on the previous page. The buildings on the left and the right with red lines match those in the present-day photo below. (photo, Atget, May 1906)

◀ Same view today. The white building in the middle on the corner of Rue de la Huchette dates from 1979.

La place du Petit-Pont, a Vestige of Petit Châtelet

From all appearances, nothing seems to distinguish this short street from any other street to earn it the name of a *place*. This distinction, though, lies in its history and not in the actual topography of the spot today.

For hundreds of years, anyone traveling into Paris from the south and wishing to reach the heart of the city on the Ile de la Cité approached from Rue Saint-Jacques and then crossed the Petit-Pont to the island. To defend this vulnerable point of entry against warring armies, a fortress known as the Petit Châtelet was constructed on the Left Bank quai. A similar but much larger defensive structure stood at the entrance to the Pont au Change on the Right Bank and was known as the Grand Châtelet. Hence today's Place du Châtelet.

During the Norman invasion of 866, the Petit Châtelet came under heavy siege. The small contingent of French soldiers left to defend the site, only twelve in number, repulsed the onslaught until

▲ The fortress Le Petit Châtelet on the Left Bank.

the Normans set fire to the fortress. The French soldiers, recognizing defeat, surrendered on the condition that their lives be spared. The Normans accepted and then executed all the soldiers except one because of his uncommon bravery. This soldier declined the gesture and chose to die with his companions. For years a plaque commemorating the valor of these soldiers was posted on the Hôtel Dieu annex that stood adjacent on Quai de Montebello.

In the early 13th century, King Philippe Auguste rebuilt the fortress in stone, but it was carried away in the flood of 1296. By the mid-14th century, the newly rebuilt fortress no longer held any strategic importance, and Charles V converted it into a prison. In 1724 it was annexed to the Hôtel Dieu. By 1769, new theories of hygiene led to a reconstruction of the quais and the demolition of this ancient site.

The demolition of this fortress-turned-hospital-annex created an open space that in fact did resemble a *place*, because it was so hemmed in on all sides. But with the demolition of the Hôtel Dieux annex in 1908 on Quai de Montebello, plus the widening of Rue du Petit-Pont, this space became just another street with nothing to distinguish it from surrounding streets. Today's name, therefore, is a reference to the history of the site and has little to do with its present configuration.

During excavations of this street, in 1842, 1908, and 1962, ancient paving stones from the original Roman road were found not far below the surface of the street.

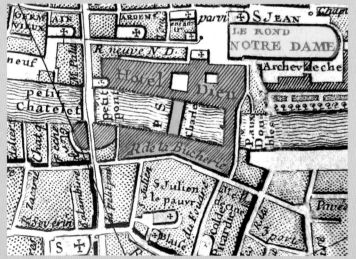

▲ Le Petit Châtelet is in blue. In red, Hôtel Dieu on Ile de la Cité with its annex on the Left Bank. In yellow, Notre Dame. (map, Delagrive, 1744)

▲ Rue du Petit-Pont looking south before widening. On the left, Rue de la Bûcherie. On the right, Rue de la Huchette. The building on the left with the red line is the same in both photos on this page. Notice it has lost its balconies. Compare the corner building on the right with the building colored blue on p. 47. (photo, Marville, 1868)

► Same view today.

Rue Saint-Séverin ⑮

▶ Rue Saint-Séverin seen from Rue Galande. On the right, a very narrow Rue du Petit-Pont before widening. On the left, Rue Saint-Jacques. The building on the left is a hotel. Behind it is the church of Saint-Séverin. The hotel and the first building on the right were demolished for street widening. Compare the building with the blue line on the right to the one in the photo on p. 46. (photo, Marville, 1867)

▼ Same view today.

▲ Street-widening projects for Rues Saint-Séverin, Galande, Saint-Julien le Pauvre, du Petit-Pont, and Saint-Jacques. Only the last three were carried out.

Rue Saint-Jacques ⑯

Rue Saint-Jacques dates back to Roman times. On the Right Bank, this thoroughfare connected to today's Rue Saint-Martin and led to the northern provinces. On the Left Bank it was the main road to Orleans in the south. The street ran along the Aqueduct of Arcueil that brought water from Rungis to the Palais des Thermes, now in ruins at the corner of Boulevard Saint-Germain and Boulevard Saint-Michel.

Once known as the Grand Rue, the street took on its present name in the 13th century because of the Chapelle des Freres Precheurs dedicated to Saint Jacques and located on Rue Cujas. During excavations for Haussmann's public works, paving stones were found under the street dating from the 4th century. Remnants of the ancient Roman *cardo* were found here as recently as 1975. Various widening projects since the late 19th century have altered the street greatly. A portion of Rue Saint-Jacques in the neighborhood of Boulevard Port-Royal retains its narrowness of ancient times.

▲ Rue Saint-Jacques. Haussmann's plans for street widening here date from 1855. They were not carried out until 1907–1908. Behind the tree is a hotel, the same as in the top photo on the previous page. Behind the hotel is the Church of Saint-Séverin. (photo, Atget, 1902)

◄ Same view today.

▲ Rue Saint-Jacques looking north. On the the left is the Church of Saint-Séverin. In the distance is a very narrow Rue du Petit-Pont. Compare to the photos on p. 50. The buildings on the left in the distance were demolished in 1907–1908 for street widening. With the exception of the first building on the right, the others on that side still stand. Compare to p. 46. (photo, Atget, 1903–1904)

▶ Same view today.

▲ Rue Saint-Jacques looking north before widening. The first street on the left is Rue de la Parcheminerie. The first building on the right, with balconies, is number 31 and was constructed in 1901. It is set back because it was thought that this side of the street, as well as the opposite side, would eventually be torn down and rebuilt on the same alignment. (photo, Atget, 1903)

◀ Same view today.

Rue de la Parcheminerie ⑰

Rue de la Parcheminerie dates from the 13th century and served as a connection between Rue de la Harpe and Rue Saint-Jacques, two main thoroughfares running north–south through Paris. The street was originally called Rue des Ecrivains because of the great number of public writers located there. The street took its present name in 1387 when it became the center of the parchment trade, an essential product in the student quarter.

In 1799, a decree signed by Napoleon Bonaparte set the width of the street at six meters (19.6 feet). In 1840 a new ordinance extended it to ten meters (32 feet). Neither of these proposals were carried out, and the street remained unchanged until 1913, when the majority of its buildings were demolished.

▶ Rue de la Parcheminerie looking west towards Rue de la Harpe. The first two buildings on the right were demolished. (postcard, private collection)

▼ The plan for widening Rue de la Parcheminerie and Rue Saint-Jacques. The odd-numbered buildings on Rue Saint-Jacques were spared demolition, as were the even-numbered buildings on Rue de la Parcheminerie.

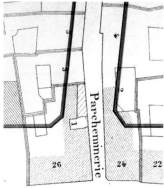

▲ Rue de la Parcheminerie, looking west. Widening is under way. (photo, Atget, 1913)

► Same view today. The first two buildings are the same as in the photo above. The building at the very end on Rue de la Harpe is the same as on the previous page.

▲ Rue de la Parcheminerie looking east towards Rue Saint-Jacques. The first building on the right is the same in both photos and is visible on the previous page, where it is the first building on the left. Everything else seen here was demolished in 1913. (photo, Atget)

▶ Same view today. The building on the right is the same as in the photo above.

▶ Rue de la Parcheminerie looking east from Rue de la Harpe. (photo, Marville, 1868)

◀ Same view today. This is the only section of this once-lively street that has remained intact. The building on the left, at 41 Rue de la Harpe, is from the early 17th century. On the right, 43 Rue de la Harpe dates from the late 17th century but was restored with a heavy hand in 1991–1992, resulting in a loss of character.

Rue de la Harpe ⓲

▲ Rue de la Harpe looking north. Before the creation of the Boulevard Saint-Michel, this narrow street, along with Rue Saint-Jacques, was a main thoroughfare north–south through Paris. (photo, Marville)

◄ Same view today. Rue de la Harpe seen from Boulevard Saint-Germain.

Rue des Prêtres-Saint-Séverin ⑲

▼ Same view today. The building that looks medieval is the church presbytery, constructed in 1926.

▲ Rue des Prêtres-Saint-Séverin. On the left, the Church of Saint-Séverin. Everything except the church was demolished for street widening. (photo, Pottier, 1904)

◄ Rue des Prêtres-Saint-Séverin looking north. Everything on the left, plus the wall on the right, has been demolished, greatly widening this narrow street.

▲ Same view today. On the right is the church presbytery, built in 1926 in a neo-Gothic style. The building on the left is visible on the next page, bottom right.

▲ Rue des Prêtres-Saint-Séverin. Demolition across the street from the presbytery. (photo, Atget, August 1914)

◄ Same street before demolition.

▼ Same view today. This enormously unattractive building, erected in 1975, is a child-care center and library.

▼ Rue des Prêtres-Saint-Séverin seen from Rue Boutebrie. The buildings are in demolition for street widening. (photo, Atget, circa 1908)

▲ Rue des Prêtres-Saint-Séverin viewed from Rue Boutebrie. The building on the left is 20 Rue de la Parcheminerie. The building on the right corner was constructed in 1861. Everything else has been demolished. The curbs in the foreground are the same in all three photos. Match the blue window to the same in the photo on the right. (photo, Marville, 1868)

► Same view today. The building on the right is visible in the photo above. The door was added later.

▼ On the corner, a grocer at 20 Rue de la Parcheminerie. In the foreground, Rue Boutebrie leading into Rue des Prêtres-Saint-Séverin. The street lamp is the same as the one in the top left photo on the previous page. (photo, Atget, 1912)

▲ Rue Boutebrie, viewed south from Rue des Prêtres-Saint-Séverin. The cross street is Rue de la Parcheminerie. Compare the street lamp with the same in the top-left photo on the previous page. The building with the red line dates from 1861 and is the same in the top and bottom photos. (photo, Atget, 1899)

◀ Same view today. The building on the right in the photo above has been demolished. Everything else still stands.

▲ Rue des Carmes from the corner of Rue de Lanneau (left) and Rue de l'Ecole-Polytechnique (right) before widening in 1923.

Boulevard Saint-Germain and Montagne Sainte-Geneviève

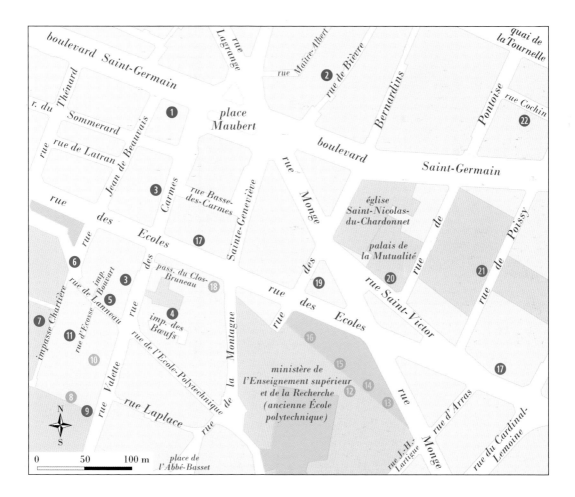

boulevard Saint-Germain

rue Lagrange

rue Maître-Albert

rue de Bièvre

②

quai de la Tournelle

r. du Thénard

Sommerard

①

place Maubert

Bernardins

Pontoise

rue Cochin

㉒

rue de Latran

Jean de Beauvais

boulevard

Saint-Germain

rue

rue Basse-des-Carmes

③

Carmes

Sainte-Geneviève

rue Monge

église Saint-Nicolas-du-Chardonnet

rue de Poissy

rue

des

Ecoles

⑰

palais de la Mutualité

⑥

imp. Bouvart

pass. du Clos-Bruneau

⑱

des

⑳

rue de

㉑

rue Chartière

rue de Lanneau

③

⑤

rue d'Ecosse

imp. des Bœufs

④

rue de la Montagne

rue

⑲

rue

des

Ecoles

rue Saint-Victor

⑦

⑪

rue de l'École-Polytechnique

⑯

⑰

⑩

rue Valette

ministère de l'Enseignement supérieur et de la Recherche (ancienne École polytechnique)

⑮

⑧

⑨

rue Laplace

rue

⑫

⑭

⑬

rue

rue d'Arras

Monge

rue J.-H.-Lartigue

rue du Cardinal-Lemoine

N

S

0   50   100 m

place de l'Abbé-Basset

Boulevard Saint-Germain ❶

When Haussmann came to power in 1853, Rue des Ecoles had already been started by Prefect Jean-Jacques Berger. Haussmann's intention was to cut a road across the Left Bank to match the Grands Boulevards on the Right Bank, creating an inner ring to facilitate traffic circulation through the city. Believing Rue des Ecoles to be too high on the hill, he discontinued work on that street and built Boulevard Saint-Germain. Dozens of old streets were erased from the map. Haussmann spared the Montagne Saint-Geneviève, although road-widening projects carried out after his departure from the Hôtel de Ville greatly altered this quarter. Boulevard Saint-Germain was created in three phases over a period of twenty-five years. The first section, completed in 1861, extended from Quai de la Tournelle to Rue Hautefeuille. The second section of the boulevard, completed around 1870, extended from Pont de la Concorde to Rue Saint-Dominique. The central portion of the boulevard was finished in 1877. Haussmann's demolition of a number of fine old townhouses in the Faubourg Saint-Germain provided ammunition for his critics.

▲ Boulevard Saint-Germain. On the left, Rue des Carmes. The buildings of old Rue des Noyers* still stand. They were torn down in the 1920s and 1930s. Compare the building with the red line to the photos on p. 71. On the extreme left is the old covered market hall, Marché des Carmes. (photo, Marville)

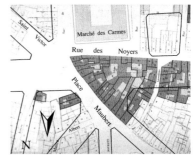

▶ In orange, buildings to be expropriated for Boulevard Saint-Germain. Rue Maître-Albert would have been lost in this plan and Rue de Bièvre widened beyond recognition.

◀ Boulevard Saint-Germain looking west from Rue Jean de Beauvais. Only the first two buildings stand today. Alfred de Musset was born in the fourth house on the left in 1810. (photo, Lansiaux, 1917)

▼ Same view today.

▼ Beautiful 17th-century wrought-iron banister inside 53 Boulevard Saint-Germain, in the second building on the left in the photo above.

Rue de Bièvre ❷

Rue de Bièvre began as a canal bringing water to the gardens of the Abbey of Saint-Victor. When the Philippe Auguste wall was surrounded by a moat in 1328, this canal, no longer serving its original purpose, became little more than a sewer. As its condition deteriorated through time, the canal was enclosed in 1672, but local residents, no longer having a place to dump their refuse, broke holes in the canal covering.

For centuries the street was a link between Quai de la Tournelle and Rue Saint-Victor. Among its famed residents were Dante, who reportedly began work on his *Divine Comedy* here in the early 14th century, and Restif le Breton in 1776.

The opening of Rue Monge and Boulevard Saint-Germain shortened Rue de Bièvre. From the map on the right it is clear that had Haussmann's plans been fully carried out, the street would have been not only shortened, but demolished and rebuilt on a wider scale.

Rue de Bièvre came close to total obliteration a second time in the 1960s as part of Ilot 3, one of the sixteen slum neighborhoods in Paris slated for total demolition. An initiative on the part of local architects interested in the preservation of French heritage saved not only the street but the whole quarter. Restoration of the street was so successful that President François Mitterand spent his last years here.

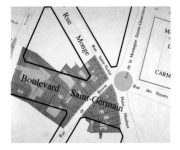

▲ The green circle indicates the old intersection of Rue Saint-Victor, Rue des Noyers*, Rue de la Montagne Sainte-Geneviève, Place Maubert, and Rue de Bièvre. The opening of Boulevard Saint-Germain eliminated this intersection and shortened Rue de Bièvre. The houses colored orange were demolished.

▼ Rue de Bièvre in 1917. How amazed these residents would be to know that one day their street would be home to the ultra-chic set.

▲ Rue de Bièvre from Boulevard Saint-Germain. The first building on the left was demolished. (photo, Marville)

◀ Same view today.

Rue des Carmes ❸

Rue des Carmes was opened in 1250 through the vineyard Clos Bruneau. Originally Rue du Clos Bruneau, it became Rue Saint-Hilaire in 1317 because it served as a path linking Rue des Noyers* to the Church of Saint-Hilaire at the corner of Rue des Carmes and Rue de Lanneau. The street took on its present name in 1322.

The Couvent des Carmes (Carmelite convent) was established at the corner of Rue des Carmes and Rue des Noyers* in 1317. The convent was closed in 1790 and demolished in 1813. The representation in the Turgot map gives a hint at the extensive loss suffered. The Marché des Carmes, fashioned after the Marché Saint-Germain, was built in its place and was completed in 1819. The market, in its turn, was demolished in 1934 to make room for the apartment building we see today. A large portion of the south side of the market was left standing and was torn down as recently as 1971. The fountain, a most important detail of the old market, stands today in the Square Gabriel Pierné in Rue Mazarine, near Métro Odéon.

▲ On the left, the Marché des Carmes, built in 1813–1819 and demolished in 1934. The building on the right is on the corner of Rue des Noyers* and Rue des Carmes and is visible in the top two photos on the next page.

▲ The fountain from Marché des Carmes in the square Gabriel Pierné in Rue Mazarine.

▶ In blue, the Carmelite convent. In red, Rue des Noyers*, today's Boulevard Saint-Germain. In green, Rue des Carmes. In orange and yellow, the 13-century wall of Philippe Auguste.

▲ The corner of Rue des Carmes and Boulevard Saint-Germain. Note the sign on the second floor advertising the services of a midwife. (photo, Godefroy)

▶ Same corner during demolition. (photo, Godefroy).

◀ Same corner today.

▲ Rue des Carmes from Boulevard Saint-Germain. On the left, the Marché des Carmes. In the distance, the Pantheon. Compare the building on the right to the photos on pp. 70 and 71, and the building with the red line to the same in the present-day photo. (photo, Godefroy)

◄ Same view today.

▲ Rue des Carmes from Rue des Ecoles, looking south, circa 1920.

▶ Same view today.

◀ Engraving of Rue des Carmes in demolition, looking south. On the right, the Collège de Beauvais. In the distance, the Pantheon.

Impasse des Bœufs ❹

▶ Impasse des Bœufs, looking west. This courtyard opens onto Rue de l'Ecole-Polytechnique. Everything has been demolished except the building on the right, the Collège des Lombards. (photo, 1917)

▼ Same view today. The brick building was constructed in 1934; its arch leads to the intersection of Rues Valette, Lanneau, Carmes, and de l'Ecole-Polytechnique.

▼ The wall of the Collège des Lombards in Impasse des Bœufs. Students residing in the building diverted themselves by cutting their names into the stone. This name, H. Conwell, dates from the 18th century.

Rue de Lanneau ❺

▼ View from corner of Rue de l'Ecole-Polytechnique. On the left, Rue Valette. The two-story building on the left was demolished in 1967. The building in its place dates from 1979. (photo, Marville)

◄ Same view today. The building on the right is in the Marville photo below.

▼ The Church of Saint-Hilaire. This church stood on the corner of Rue des Carmes and Rue de Lanneau. Built in the 13th century, it was confiscated during the Revolution, sold in 1795, and demolished in 1807. In 1513, a great dispute broke out in the church between two men arguing over whether Adam and Eve, having no mother, should be represented with belly buttons. The dispute came to blows. Vestiges of the church have been incorporated into the building at 1 Rue de Lanneau.

▲ Rue de Lanneau looking west. It opened around 1185 as Rue Saint-Hilaire. By 1571, this short street had fourteen booksellers. On the left, Rue d'Ecosse. At the end of the street, Impasse Chartière. This street would have been entirely demolished had the plan for cutting a new street through here been carried out. (postcard, private collection)

◄ Same view today. Note the sidewalks have been eliminated.

Intersection of Impasse Chartière and Rues Jean de Beauvais, de Lanneau, Fromental*, and Saint-Jean de Latran* ⑥

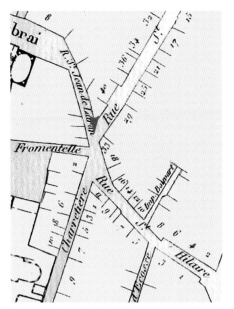

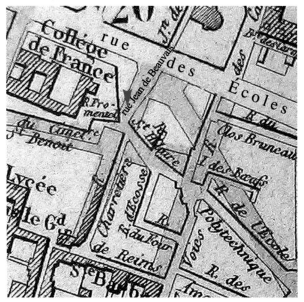

▲ In yellow, proposed new streets. Rue Saint-Hilaire (today's Rue de Lanneau) would have been erased. The arrow in both maps represents the point of view of the photo below. (map, Andriveau Goujon, 1863)

◄ Intersection of Rues Jean de Beauvais and Saint-Jean de Latran*. Compare the building with the red line to the same one on p. 78. Behind it is Rue Fromental*. In the distance, Impasse Chartière goes off to the right and Rue de Lanneau to the left. (photo, Marville)

▲ Rue des Ecoles has not yet been cut through. The buildings on the right were demolished in order to enlarge the Collège de France in the 1930s. The first buildings on the left were demolished to open Rue des Ecoles. The building with the red line is the same as on the previous page. (photo, Emonts, 1869)

▶ Same view today. In the foreground, Rue des Ecoles. Straight ahead, Rue Jean de Beauvais leading to Impasse Chartière.

▼ Door on Impasse Chartière, to the left of the woman holding the child in the photo on the left.

▲ Intersection of Rue de Lanneau (left), Impasse Chartière (right), and Rue Fromental* (hard right). (photo, Lansiaux)

► Same view today.

▼ Same view today. To the right, Place Maurice-Berthelot.

▲ On the left, Impasse Chartière. On the right, Rue Saint-Jean de Latran. In the middle lies the beginning of Rue Fromental*. Match the facade with the red line to the photo from two pages previous. All these buildings were demolished in the 1930s in order to enlarge the Collège de France. (photo, Lansiaux)

Impasse Chartière ❼

▼ Impasse Chartière towards the intersection with Rue de Lanneau.

▲ Same view today. Note the building at the end of the street in the photo to the right is gone today.

Rue de Reims*⑧

► A view of Rue de Reims towards Rue Chartière as seen from Rue des Sept-Voies, later Rue Valette. This street was demolished in 1880–1882 so that the Collège Sainte-Barbe could be enlarged. Match the red line on the right to the same in the Marville photo on the next page. (photo, Marville, 1865)

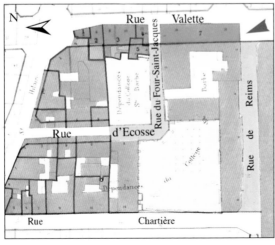

◄ Map showing plan to widen Rue Valette. In blue, two streets eliminated for enlarging Collège Sainte-Barbe. This project made dead ends out of two streets, Rue d'Ecosse and Impasse Chartière. The red arrow indicates the same building marked in red in the photo above and on the next page.

Rue Valette ❾

▲ Rue Valette looking north. On the left, Rue de Reims*. The building with the red line matches the building on the right on the previous page. The arched entryway on the right is the same in the photo below. (photo, Marville)

▶ Same view today.

Rue du Four-Saint-Jacques*⑩

◀ Rue Valette. The building also appears in the photo below.

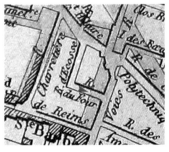

▶ Rue du Four-Saint-Jacques seen from Rue d'Ecosse, looking towards Rue des Sept-Voies, today Rue Valette. The former was eliminated for the enlargement of the Collège de France. The facade at the end of the street is on Rue Valette and still stands. (photo, Marville, 1868)

Rue d'Ecosse ⑪

◀ Rue d'Ecosse. Looking towards Rue Saint-Hilaire, today's Rue de Lanneau. This street was cut in half and made into a dead end when the Collège de France was enlarged and the Rue du Four-Saint-Jacques was eliminated. (photo, Marville, 1865)

▼ Same view today.

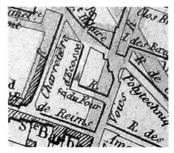

Rue Traversine* ⑫

Rue Traversine* and the surrounding streets, many dating from the Middle Ages, formed one of the oldest quarters in pre-Haussmann Paris. The opening of Rue Monge and Rue des Ecoles erased it all from the map. Rue des Ecoles was laid out in several phases from 1853 to 1868. This street was begun by Prefect Jean-Jacques Berger and was to cut straight across the Left Bank. When Haussmann came to power, he considered this thoroughfare to be too high on the hill. He preferred to build closer to the river and thus discontinued Rue des Ecoles and began Boulevard Saint-Germain.

Rue Monge was built between 1859 and 1864. In the Square Paul-Langevin at the intersection of Rue Monge and Rue des Ecoles, one can see the 18th-century fountain that formerly stood at the opening of old Rue Childebert*, demolished for Boulevard Saint-Germain.

▲ Rue Traversine* looking west. On the right, Rue Fresnel*, formerly Rue de Versailles*. On the left, Impasse de Versailles*. The blue lamp is the same as the one on p. 88. This street runs along the wall of the Ecole Polytechnique in the Square Paul-Langevin today. (photo, Marville)

◀▶ This rectangle was formerly crossed by Rues du Mûrier* (in blue), du Paon* (in red), du Bon-Puits* (in orange), and de Versailles* (in green), all perpendicular to Rue Traversine*. They were erased for the creation of Rues Monge and des Ecoles. In dark blue at the top, the Church of Saint-Nicolas-du-Chardonnet. (map on the left, Hérisson, 1822)

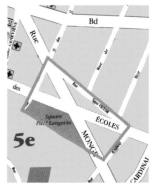

◄ Square Paul-Langevin at the intersection of Rue Monge and Rue des Ecoles. On the left is the wall of the Ecole Polytechnique. Old Rue Traversine* ran along the wall. At right angles to it ran Rues du Mûrier*, du Paon*, du Bon-Puits*, and Fresnel*, de Versailles*.

► Rue des Ecoles cutting through four medieval streets. Rue Monge, in yellow, will finish them off.

▼ Rue des Ecoles and Rue Monge superimposed over Rue du Bon-Puits, Rue Fresnel*, de Versailles*, Rue du Paon*, and Rue du Mûrier*. In green, today's Square Paul-Langevin. At the top in blue, Impasse de Versailles*.

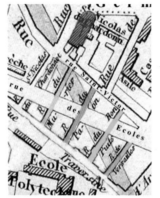

▼ Childebert fountain. Built in 1715, it originally stood at the opening of Rue Childebert near the Church of Saint-Germain-des-Prés. It was relocated to Square Paul-Langevin when the boulevard was cut through.

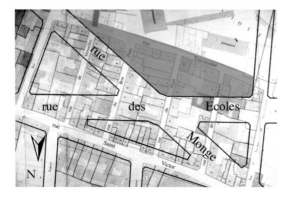

Rue Fresnel* ⓭

▶ Rue Fresnel*, formerly Rue de Versailles*, from Impasse de Versailles*, looking towards Rue Saint-Victor. The first cross street is Rue Traversine*. Rue Fresnel* was demolished in 1859 for Rue Monge. Compare the blue lamp to the one on p. 86. (photo, Marville)

Rue du Bon-Puits*⓮

▼ Rue du Bon-Puits* from Rue Traversine* towards Rue Saint-Victor. (photo, Marville)

Rue du Paon*⑮

▶ Rue du Paon* from Rue Saint-Victor towards Rue Traversine*. (photo, Marville)

Rue du Mûrier* ⑯

◄ Rue du Mûrier* from Rue Traversine* towards Rue Saint-Victor. The building at the end of the street is the Seminary of Saint-Nicolas-du-Chardonnet. Compare to pp. 98–99. (photo, Marville)

Rue des Ecoles ⓱

▶ View east from Rue des Ecoles. On the immediate left, Rue du Cardinal Lemoine. The second left is Rue des Fossés-Saint-Bernard. Straight ahead, Rue Jussieu and the Halles aux Vins, today the site of the Jussieu Campus of the Faculty of Sciences of the University of Paris VI and VII. The building on the left still stands. (photo, Marville)

▼ Same view today.

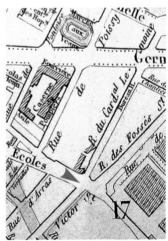

▲ Rue Traversine* east from Rue de la Montagne Sainte-Geneviève. These buildings were demolished for the creation of Rue Monge. (photo, Marville, 1865)

▼ Same view today. Rue des Ecoles is straight ahead. On the right, Rue de la Montagne Sainte-Geneviève.

▼ 21 and 23 Rue des Ecoles today. Two buildings from old Rue Traversine*, remarkably still standing.

Rue du Clos-Bruneau*⑱

▲ In the foreground is a new Rue des Ecoles, as yet without buildings. On the left, Rue de la Montagne Sainte-Geneviève. The buildings outlined in red stand in today's Passage du Clos-Bruneau. Everything else has been demolished. (photo, Marville)

▼ Same view today.

◄ In the foreground, Rue des Ecoles. The upper-level street is Rue du Clos-Bruneau*, eliminated in 1855 for Rue des Ecoles. The building with the blue line is today's 13 Passage du Clos-Bruneau. (photo, Marville, circa 1855)

▼ Same view today. On the extreme left, 27 Rue des Ecoles. Compare to the Marville photo above. The arch leads into Passage du Clos-Bruneau and is in the same place as the staircase in the Marville photo.

◄◄ Passage du Clos-Bruneau from Rue des Ecoles. The green house at the top of the stairs is the small house on the left within the red outline in the photo above. The stairway was added some years after the new building was in place. It is believed a butcher shop stood here originally. But people living in Passage du Clos-Bruneau complained of their street being not only amputated but also left with only one means of entry. To appease them, the city tore down the butcher shop and constructed this stairway leading onto Rue des Ecoles.

Rue Saint-Nicolas-du-Chardonnet ⑲

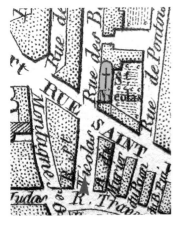

▶ Rue Saint-Nicolas-du-Chardonnet (today Rue des Bernardins) looking towards Rue Saint-Victor from Rue des Ecoles. Down the street, on the right, the Church of Saint-Nicolas-du-Chardonnet. (photo, Marville, 1860)

▼ Same view today from Rue des Ecoles.

Rue Saint-Victor 20

Rue Saint-Victor was created in the 12th century as a path connecting Place Maubert to the Abbey of Saint-Victor. It was later extended to the Porte Saint-Victor at the Philippe Auguste fortification that encircled Paris. The opening of Rue des Ecoles in 1855 demolished a large part of the street. The coup de grâce came in 1864 with the opening of Rue Monge. The 17th-century seminary of Saint-Nicolas-du-Chardonnet was one of the few buildings spared from demolition, but it too fell in 1914. Today the Palais de la Mutualité stands in its place. Only eight houses remain of this once-vibrant thoroughfare.

► Rue Saint-Victor looking towards Place Maubert. The entire street is still intact. The first cross street is Rue des Bernardins. The left side of the street was demolished first for the creation of Rue Monge. Between the red lines on the right is the entry into the Church of Saint-Nicolas-du-Chardonnet. (photo, Marville, 1865)

▼ Same view today.

► Rue Saint-Victor in its entirety between red lines. In blue, the only portion remaining today. In light green, the church of Saint-Nicolas-du-Chardonnet.

◄ Rue Saint-Victor looking east. Charles Marville simply turned his camera around to shoot this photo. On the left, the Seminary of Saint-Nicolas-du-Chardonnet, constructed between 1684 and 1687, closed in 1906, and demolished in 1914. Compare to pp. 91 and the next page. (photo, Marville)

► Same view today. On the left, the Palais de la Mutualité.

►► The Seminary of Saint-Nicolas-du-Chardonnet in demolition.

▲ Rue Saint-Victor in 1869. The buildings that stood opposite the seminary have been demolished for the creation of Rue Monge. Note the church on the left behind the buildings. Match the red lines to the same on p. 97. (photo, Emonts)

▼ Same view today. The new entry to the church was completed in the 1930s.

Collège des Bernardins

The Collège des Bernardins was established in 1246 by the Cistercian order of the Abbey of Clairveux. Large building projects begun in 1338 by the Cistercian Pope, Benoit XII, extended the domain of the monastery from the Seine to Rue Saint-Victor and from Rue des Bernardins to Rue Cardinal-Lemoine. The church begun during this period was never finished and stood lacking its facade. Surrounding the monastery was an eight-meter (8.75-yard) wall, an encouragement to student contemplation and a discouragement to their seeking diversion elsewhere.

In 1772–1774, as the monastery lost its preeminence, a large part of the gardens was ceded to the city for the Halle aux Veaux and the opening of Rue de Pontoise and Rue de Poissy. During the Revolution the entire site was nationalized (1790), and in 1797 the church chapel was demolished.

The refectory, the largest standing remnant of the monastery, was given to the city in 1805. In 1845 this gem of Gothic architecture was temporarily converted into a firehouse. This situation, degrading to the site, continued until 1993. In 2004 the city of Paris undertook a massive project to restore the refectory to its former glory. It was completed in fall 2007, and today the site is open to the pubic.

▲ Collège des Bernardins looking north.

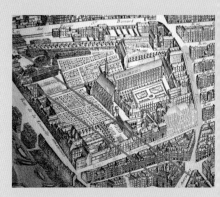

▶ Collège des Bernardins. In blue, refectory. Between the red lines lies the future path of Boulevard Saint-Germain. The orange line follows the curve of Rue Saint-Victor. In green, Rue des Bernardins. (Turgot map, 18th century)

▼ The cellar under the eastern wing of the Collège des Bernardins. (© Emmanuel Gaffard)

Rue de Poissy ㉑

▼ Remnant of Collège des Bernardins, today part of the apartment buildings on Boulevard Saint-Germain. (photo, Godefroy)

▲ Vestiges of the Collège des Bernardins. The fence on the lower left runs along a new Boulevard Saint-Germain, as yet without buildings, today's 25 to 33 Boulevard Saint-Germain. The red line is on Rue du Poissy. (photo, Godefroy)

▲ Same view today on Boulevard Saint-Germain.

◄ The refectory of the Collège des Bernardins on Rue de Poissy. Converted "temporarily" into a firehouse in 1845, it remained so until 1993.

Rue Cochin ㉒

The Halle aux Veaux was established here in 1772 on the former grounds of the Collège des Bernardins. Rues de Pontoise and de Poissy, designed as access roads to the market, originally ran from Rue Cochin almost to today's Boulevard Saint-Germain. They were extended to Rue Saint-Victor in 1802. The market stood on this spot until the 1860s, when it was moved to La Villette in the north of Paris.

▲ Rue Cochin looking east from Rue de Pontoise. On the right, Halle aux Veaux. In this photo the market has been moved, but the structure remains. (photo, Marville)

▼ Same view today.

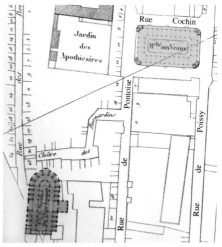

▲ The Church of Saint-Nicolas-du-Chardonnet is in red. The Halle aux Veaux is in blue, before the construction of Boulevard Saint-Germain.

▶▶ The church of Saint-Nicolas-du-Chardonnet (in red) and the Halle aux Veaux (in blue), separated by the Boulevard Saint-Germain laid out by Haussmann.

▲ Halle aux Veaux viewed from Rue de Pontoise towards Boulevard Saint-Germain. The street on the left corresponds to Rue Cochin. The market was built in 1772. (photo, Marville, 1865)

► Same view today.

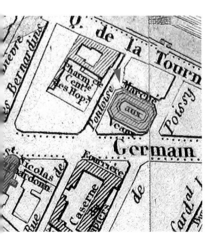

▲ Place Gozlin (today's Place d'Acadie, better known as Place Mabillon), looking north from Rue du Four. The balcony on the lower left is at the corner of Rue du Four and Boulevard Saint-Germain. On the left, Rue de l'Echaudé. On the right, Rue de Buci.

From Odéon to Saint-Germain-des-Prés

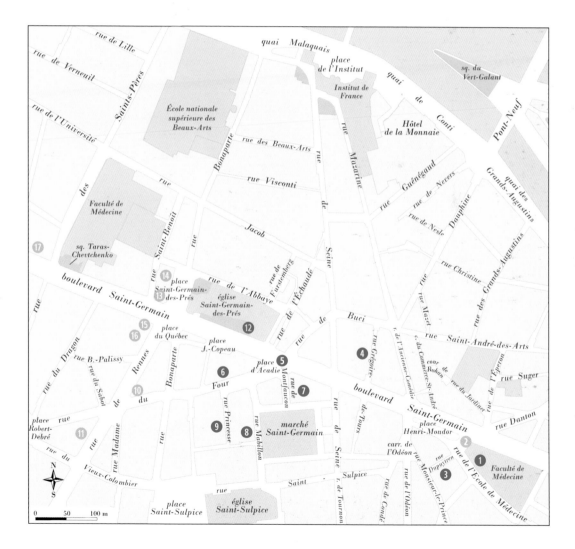

Extension of Boulevard Saint-Germain

In 1863 Boulevard Saint-Germain stopped at Rue Hautefeuille shortly after it crossed Boulevard Saint-Michel. The creation of the latter erased a number of streets that gave this quarter its particular character. Rue de la Harpe, in pink in the right-hand map below, was a major traffic artery crossing the Left Bank from north to south from Place Saint-Michel. Much of this street was absorbed by Boulevard Saint-Michel. The extension of Boulevard Saint-Germain to Quai d'Orsay, completed in 1878, erased a part of Rue du Jardinet and Rue and Impasse Larrey* (formerly Rue and Impasse du Paon*), altered Rue Hautefeuille, in green, and shortened Rue de l'Ecole de Médecine, leaving only the portion east of Place Henri-Mondor, in blue.

◀ Rue Hautefeuille. A portion of this street, numbers 20–24 at the curve, was lost for the opening of Boulevard Saint-Germain.

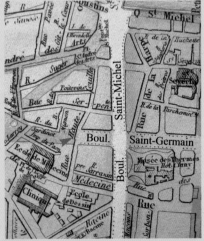

▲ Boulevard Saint-Germain stopping at Rue Hautefeuille. (map, 1863)

Rue de l'Ecole de Médecine ➊

▼ Same view. Place Henri-Mondor.

▲ Rue de l'Ecole de Médecine. Photo taken from window of Jean-Paul Marat's tower. See p. 109. In the distance, the steeple of the Church of Saint-Germain-des-Prés. (photo, Emonts, 1875)

◄◄ This map shows pre-Haussmann Paris and the maze of narrow streets the population had to negotiate. In pink, a narrow Rue de la Harpe, one of two main thoroughfares along with Rue Saint-Jacques, for cutting north–south through Paris.

► Rue de l'Ecole de Médecine. Only
the buildings on the right exist.
Everything else was demolished for the
creation of Boulevard Saint-Germain. In
blue on the left, the entrance to Cour
du Commerce-Sainte-André, where
Danton of the Revolution lived. (photo,
Emonts, 1875)

▼ Same view today.

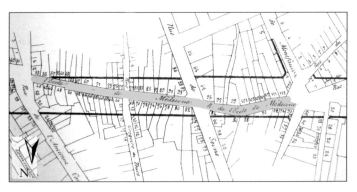

◄ In black, Boulevard Saint-Germain
cutting through old Paris. In red, Rue de
l'Ecole de Médecine extending from
Odéon on the left to Place Gozlin
(today's Place d'Acadie, better known as
Place Mabillon), on the right.

▼ Charlotte Corday apprehended after stabbing Marat in his bath.

▲ Rue de l'Ecole de Médecine. First left, Rue Larrey*. On the left, in orange, the Cordelier fountain. The house with the turret was Jean-Paul Marat's residence; he was stabbed in his bath there by Charlotte Corday on July 12, 1793. Compare to p. 107. In blue at the end of the street is the Faculty of Medicine, the only building still standing. The houses on the extreme right were demolished in 1902. Everything else was demolished earlier in 1876. (photo, Marville)

► Same view today.

Rue Larrey*❷

► Rue Larrey* from Rue de l'Ecole de Médecine. Marat's house is on the right in the foreground.

▼ Same view today.

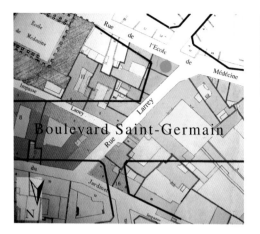

▲ Boulevard Saint-Germain cutting through the old city, obliterating Rue and Impasse Larrey* and a part of Rue du Jardinet. The green circle indicates Marat's house.

▲ Rue Larrey* looking towards Rue de l'Ecole de Médecine. The first left is Impasse Larrey*. Everything in the foreground was demolished for Boulevard Saint-Germain, which cuts through here at right angles. Marat's house is at the end of the street on the left. (photo, Godefroy)

◄ Impasse Larrey*. (photo, Godefroy)

Rue Dupuytren ❸

▶ Rue Dupuytren is on the left. In the foreground, Rue de l'Ecole de Médicine. These houses were demolished in 1902. The green circle indicates the location of Marat's house. (photo, UPF)

▼ Same view today.

Rue Grégoire-de-Tours ❹

▼ Same view today. The two buildings on the corners in the archival photo were demolished. The buildings in this photo are newer, constructed when Boulevard Saint-Germain was created.

▲ Rue Grégoire-de-Tours from Rue de l'Ecole de Médecine towards Rue de Buci. Notice the narrow street on the left lined in red (Rue de l'Ecole de Médecine). Charles Marville took this photo on the spot where a building had been torn down. The outline is still visible on the ground. (photo, Marville, circa 1868)

Place d'Acadie ⑤

▼ Today's Place d'Acadie, commonly known as Place Mabillon, was formerly known as Place Gozlin and earlier yet, as on this map, as Place Sainte-Marguerite. In green, the Church of Saint-Germain-des-Prés. In blue, the abbey prison that stood in front of today's 168 Boulevard Saint-Germain; it was demolished in 1854. In pink, the building with a vertical green line in the contemporary photo on the right. In yellow, the building with the red window in the Marville photo below. The red arrow on the right shows the point of view of the photo below. The red arrow on the left shows the point of view of the Emonts photo on the next page.

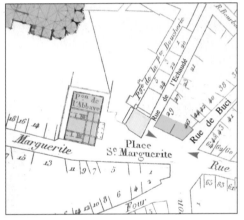

▲ Boulevard Saint-Germain. The first right is Rue de Buci. The vertical green line on the corner of the building corresponds to the building on the left of the photo below.

▶ Place Gozlin looking west from Rue de l'Ecole de Médecine. On the left, Rue du Four Saint-Germain. In the center, straight ahead is Rue Gozlin, formerly Rue Sainte-Marguerite. On the right, Rue de Buci. The only building still standing in this photo is on the far right with the vertical green line. The photo on the next page was taken from the window colored red here. Match the lamps colored blue in both photos. The red line on the left is over the door to a billiard hall, also visible on the next page. (photo, Marville, 1865)

◄ Rue de l'Ecole de Médecine. The first street on the left is Rue de Buci. In the distance is Rue de Seine. This section of Boulevard Saint-Germain was created after Haussmann left office in 1870 as prefect. His successors went against his wishes and conserved the buildings on the left between these two streets. Everything on the right was demolished for the opening of the boulevard. The red line on the right is over the entrance to a pool hall. Compare to the photo with the red line on the previous page. This photo was taken from the red window on the previous page. The building with the vertical green line matches the building on the extreme left in the photo below. Compare the dormer colored yellow to the same in the contemporary photo below. (photo, Emonts, 1868)

► Same view today. The new boulevard retained a length of pre-Haussmann buildings.

Rue du Four ⑥

▲ Rue du Four from Place Gozlin before Boulevard Saint-Germain was cut through. Rue de Montfaucon is on the left. The building on the left is also visible on pp. 118 and 119.

Rue du Four extends from Place d'Acadie to Carrefour de la Croix-Rouge (Place Michel-Debré) and is one of the oldest streets in the quarter of Saint-Germain. This important thoroughfare in the center of Paris was widened several times between 1843 and 1913.

▲ Rue du Four, looking east from Rue de Rennes.

▶ Plan of enlargement of the street east of rue de Rennes.

▼ Same view today. Compare building to the right of the red line in both photos.

▲ Rue du Four from Rue de Montfaucon. Compare the building with wrought-iron balconies on the right with the same in the photo below. (photo, Emonts, 1895)

▼ Same view today.

▼ Rue du Four in 1914. The buildings in orange are to be demolished for street widening. The proposed widening of Rue des Ciseaux was never carried out. The streets at the bottom of the map (Rue de Montfaucon, Rue Mabillon, Rue Princesse, and Rue des Canettes) were all widened as indicated.

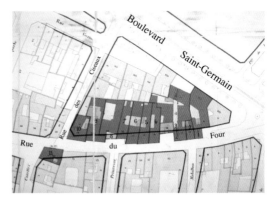

▲ The intersection of Rue de Montfaucon (on the left) and Rue du Four (on the right). The restaurant is the same as on the preceding page. This building and an identical building facing it were constructed by Pierre Boscry in the 1720s as part of Passage Bissy leading to the Foire Saint-Germain. The passage became a street in 1817 to connect with the new Marché Saint-Germain constructed by Blondel in 1813–1818. All the buildings pictured here were demolished when Rue de Montfaucon and Rue du Four were widened. (photo, Berthaud Bros., 1913)

◄ Same view today. The red line approximates the position of the building in the photo above.

Rue de Montfaucon ❼

▼ Same view today.

▲ View of 2 and 4 Rue de Montfaucon. This building, the same as those pictured on the previous page, was part of Passage Bissy. It was demolished in the early 20th century. (photo, Berthaud Bros.)

▲ View of 3 and 5 Rue de Montfaucon towards Boulevard Saint-Germain. This building was almost twice as long but was shortened for the construction of Boulevard Saint-Germain. (photo, Lansiaux, August 31, 1917)

▼ Same view today.

Rue Mabillon ⑧

▼ Same view today.

▲ Rue Mabillon from Rue du Four looking towards Marché Saint-Germain. Everything has been demolished except the market structure at the end of the street. In the 1990s, developers wanted to tear down the market and erect an apartment building. Vigorous neighborhood protests killed this proposal. As a compromise, the structure was developed as a mini–shopping mall devoid of interest. (photo, Marville)

Rue Princesse ⑨

▼ Rue Princesse from Rue du Four-Saint-Germain looking towards Rue Guisarde. Almost everything here was demolished. (photo, Marville, circa 1865)

▶ Same view today.

Rue de l'Egout*⑩

◀ Rue du Four-Saint-Germain looking west from Rue Bonaparte. The first street on the right with the red line is Rue de l'Egout*. Compare this photo to the bottom photo on the next page. (photo, Marville circa 1865)

▼ Same view today. In the distance is Rue de Rennes.

▼ Stair at 32 Rue du Four. This shows the slope mentioned on the next page. For some reason this street escaped the massive leveling Haussmann carried out around Paris.

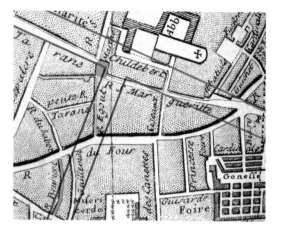

▶ Purple lines (Boulevard Saint-Germain) and black lines (Rue de Rennes) show Haussmann's new city laid out over the medieval network of streets. Erased from the map were the Saint-Benoit intersection in red (see p. 130), Rue de l'Egout* in blue, and Rue Beurrière* in green. Cour du Dragon*, in orange, stood until 1926.

▲ Same view today. Formerly Rue de l'Egout* crossed Rue du Four at this point. Off to the left is Rue de Rennes.

◀ Looking north from Rue du Four-Saint-Germain. Straight ahead is the Saint-Benoît intersection*. Note how the street slopes down and compare to page 130. Everything here was demolished for Rue de Rennes. (photo, Marville)

Rue Beurrière*⑪

▼ Rue Beurrière*, seen here from Rue du Four, was also lost to Rue de Rennes.

Boulevard Saint-Germain ⑫

▲ Boulevard Saint-Germain, partially completed, arriving at Rue d'Erfurth*. The central part of the boulevard has not yet been started. On the right, a new Haussmann building. On the left, the Church of Saint-Germain-des-Prés. The street on this side of the island on the right is Rue de Rennes. Rue Bonaparte is between the lamp and the building. (photo, Emonts)

▶ Same view today. The building on the right is the same in both photos.

Rue Sainte-Marthe* ⓭

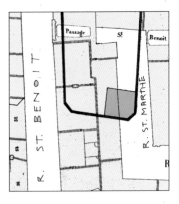

▲ Black lines show new Haussmann buildings over old Paris. In blue, Café Les Deux Magots.

▲ Rue Sainte-Marthe*. On the right, Rue Childebert*. Everything here was demolished for the construction of Boulevard Saint-Germain. Note the sign reading SPECIALITE at the end of the street and match to the photo on the next page. The Café Les Deux Magots is situated in the middle of this street.

◄ Café Les Deux Magots at the corner of Boulevard Saint-Germain and Place Saint-Germain-des-Prés.

Passage Saint-Benoît*⑭

◀ Passage Saint-Benoît* leading from Rue Sainte-Marthe* to Rue Saint-Benoît. On the right, note the SPECIALITE sign also visible on the previous page. A wine shop can be seen through the passageway on Rue Saint-Benoît. (photo, Marville)

Saint-Benoît Intersection*⑮

The Saint-Benoît intersection* was the junction of four streets: Rue Saint-Benoît, Rue Taranne*, Rue de l'Egout*, and Rue Gozlin. Comparing 19th-century photos of this intersection to today's corner of Rue de Rennes and Boulevard Saint-Germain clearly conveys Haussmann's broad vision of a modern, efficient Paris bursting through the skin of an ancient, medieval city.

◀ Saint-Benoît intersection* seen from Rue Saint-Benoît. The lamp colored blue on the far building is on the corner of Rue Gozlin on the left, and Rue de l'Egout* straight ahead. Notice how Rue de l'Egout* slopes down and compare to p. 125. See the red lamp in the photo on the next page. (photo, Marville)

▼ Boulevard Saint-Germain (right) and Rue de Rennes (straight ahead). This is a close approximation to the location of the Saint-Benoît intersection*.

▼ Saint-Benoît intersection* outlined in red. In black, Boulevard Saint-Germain and Rue de Rennes.

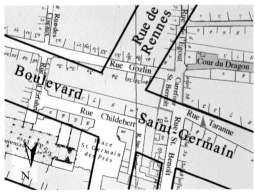

▲ Rue Taranne* (today's Boulevard Saint-Germain) from the Saint-Benoît intersection*. On the right lies Rue Saint-Benoît. The first building on the left was demolished. The next building was spared and today is the Brasserie Lipp, indicated by the red arrow. Compare the red lamp to the photo on the previous page. (photo, Marville)

◄ Boulevard Saint-Germain. The blue line separates Haussmann buildings to the left from pre-Haussmann buildings to the right. The red line indicates where the corner building with the red lamp stood on the old Saint-Benoît intersection*.

Cour
du Dragon* ⑯

► Cour du Dragon* courtyard on Rue de l'Egout*. Notice the downward slope. Cour du Dragon* miraculously survived Haussmann's opening of Rue de Rennes, only to be demolished by a later generation of barbarians. On the left, Rue Gozlin. The blue lamp is also visible in the distance on p. 130. (photo, Marville)

▼◄ The Monoprix at 50 Rue de Rennes was built in 1958 on the spot where the Cour du Dragon* formerly stood. The facade was redone in a more Haussmann style in the 1990s. The dragon on the redone entry is a replica of the original, which hangs in the Louvre.

▲ Cour du Dragon* courtyard. Built in 1732, it was torn down in 1926.

Rue Saint-Dominique*⑰

► Rue Saint-Dominique* from Rue des Saint-Pères. (photo, Marville)

▼ These buildings are the same as in the Marville photo. Compare the windows: there are five across in the first building and three across in the second.

►► Boulevard Saint-Germain, outlined in red, eliminated Rue Saint-Dominique* and Rue Taranne*. The buildings in dark orange were demolished. The two buildings visible on the right in the photo above are shaded green. The black dot is the corner building with the red lamp in the photo above.

◄ On the right, Rue Saint-Dominique* viewed from Rue des Saints-Pères. The red line on the left, the end of Rue Taranne*, is now Boulevard Saint-Germain. Compare the lamp colored red to the one on the previous page. (photo, Marville)

▼ Same view today. The building on the extreme right is the same as the one in the photo above. The building on the left is on Boulevard Saint-Germain and was part of old Rue Taranne*.

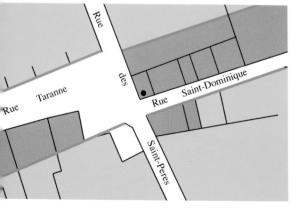

▲ Rue Beaubourg, view north. The first left is Rue de Venise. (photo, Atget, May 1899)

Rue Beaubourg and Nearby Streets

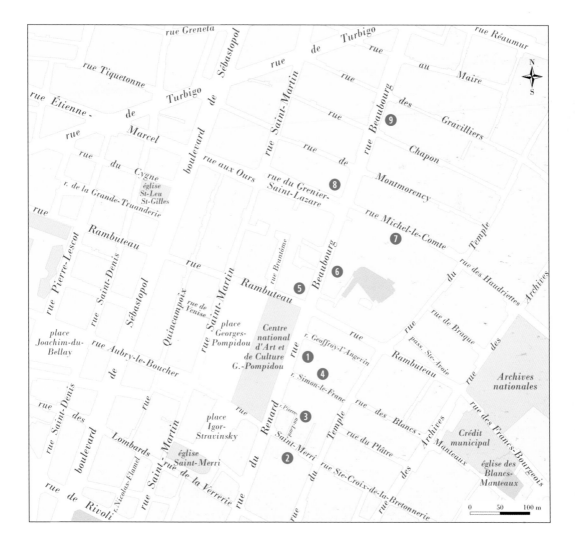

Rue Beaubourg ❶

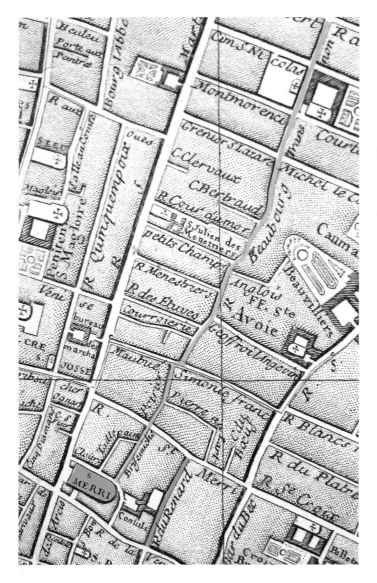

Today's Rue Beaubourg is a relatively recent addition to the geography of Paris and dates only from the early 1900s. Previously it was one segment of a narrow, winding street dating from the 11th century that began at the Church of Saint-Merri and ran north to Saint-Martin-des-Champs, later to become the Conservatoire National des Arts et Metiers. Demolition for the new thoroughfare began in 1908. Rue du Renard was widened and realigned in 1913 in order to be joined to the new Rue Beaubourg. The last demolitions in the street took place in the mid-1970s for the Quartier de l'Horloge on Rue Rambuteau. The only remaining buildings of old Rue Beaubourg are on the west side of the street from around Rue Montmorency to Rue au Maire.

▲ In blue, a medieval thoroughfare made up of Rues Brisemiche, Poirier, and Beaubourg connecting the Church of Saint-Merri and the Abbey Saint-Martin-des-Champs. In green, Rue de Renard. The two were aligned in the early 20th century to make one thoroughfare.

▲ 13 and 17 Rue Beaubourg from Rue Geoffrey l'Angevin. These buildings survived earlier demolitions in the neighborhood but were torn down in 1934 as part of a block of houses tagged a slum by the city. The vast space emptied of houses became a parking lot for the many workers laboring at the central market of Les Halles. Years later the Pompidou Center was built on the spot. (photo, Atget, 1914)

▼ Rue Beaubourg looking south. In the distance, Notre Dame. On the right, the Pompidou Center.

▼ Rue Beaubourg, looking north. On the left, the Pompidou Center.

Rue Saint-Merri ❷

▼ 16, 18, and 20 Rue Saint-Merri from Rue du Renard. The only building standing is number 16, to the right of the red line. Compare to the photo on the right. (photo, UPF, circa 1900)

▶ Same view today.

▲ 20, 22, and 24 Rue Saint-Merri from Rue Renard. Note the bearded man in the archway and find him on the left of the bottom photo on the previous page. Everything here stood in the middle of today's realigned Rue Beaubourg and Rue du Renard and has been demolished. (photo, UPF, circa 1900)

Rue Pierre-au-Lard ❸

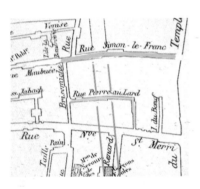

▲ Rue Pierre-au-Lard and Rue Simon-le-Franc will be cut in two by the extension of Rue du Renard.

▲ Rue Pierre-au-Lard towards Rue Brisemiche. (photo, Atget, 1908)

◀ Same view today, looking toward Rue du Renard and the Pompidou Center.

▲ 9, 11, and 13 Rue Pierre-au-Lard. Note the empty space on the right. The bottom photo was taken from that spot towards the facade on the left side of this photo. This section of the street was demolished for the reconfiguration of Rue du Renard. (photo, UPF, circa 1900)

▶ 13 Rue Pierre-au-Lard circa 1900, viewed from the empty lot where a building was torn down. (photo, UPF)

Rue Simon-le-Franc ④

▲ 18 Rue Simon-le-Franc from Rue du Renard. Everything here was demolished. (photo, Gossin, 1913)

◄ 20 Rue Simon-le-Franc. January, 1913.

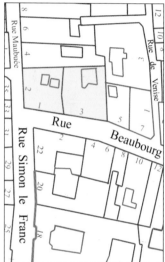

◄ On the right, the door to 20 Rue Simon-le-Franc corresponds to the red line on the map. At the corner are 1 and 3 Rue Beaubourg, in blue on the map. Everything here was demolished for widening of Rue Beaubourg. (photo, Atget, March 1914)

▼ Same view today. Rue Simon-le-Franc towards Rue Beaubourg and the Pompidou Center.

Rue
Rambuteau ❺

► The corner of Rue Rambuteau, running left and right, and Rue Beaubourg, going off to the left behind the striped awning, circa 1900. Everything here was demolished for street widening. (photo, Musée Carnavalet)

▼ Rue Beaubourg from Rue Rambuteau. The red circle corresponds to the arrow on the map.

▲ A widened Rue Beaubourg obliterates the older, narrower street. The arrow corresponds to the point of view of the photo above.

▲ Rue Rambuteau. The buildings to the left of the red line were demolished in order to widen Rue Beaubourg. The building to the right of the red line still stands. (photo, Musée Carnavalet)

◄ Same view today. Rue Beaubourg is on the left and Rue Rambuteau on the right. Compare the balcony with the blue line to the same in the older photo.

▲ Rue Beaubourg. The red line denotes a restaurant at number 29, Rendez-vous des Routiers, just before demolition. Compare to the top photo on the next page. (photo, Marc Petitjean, 1975)

▶ Same view today.

▲ Rue Beaubourg at Rue Rambuteau. The Pompidou Center is under construction. The building with the red line is number 29. (photo, Marc Petitjean, 1974)

◄ Same view today.

Rue Beaubourg ⑥

▲ Rue Beaubourg in April 1898. The red line marks number 29, later the restaurant Rendez-Vous des Routiers, which is visible on the previous two pages. The narrow street to the right of this building is Rue Brantôme*. (photo, UPF)

▶ These buildings at 25, 27, 29 Rue Beaubourg await their fate, part of the demolition seen here for the future Quartier de l'Horloge. The ancient Rue Brantôme*, to the right of these buildings, has been erased from the map. (photo, Marc Petitjean, 1975)

◄ Rue Beaubourg. The restaurant at number 29 awaits demolition for the future Quartier de l'Horloge. (photo, Marc Petitjean, 1975)

▼ Same view today: Quartier de l'Horloge on Rue Beaubourg. The building with the dome is the same in both photos.

▲ The courtyard of 29 Rue Beaubourg, lost to demolition. (photo, Marc Petitjean, 1975)

▲ Rue Beaubourg looking south. The first buildings on the right are numbers 39 to 43. The first right is Impasse Beaubourg. In the 13th century, the Philippe Auguste fortification cut across here.

◄ Rue Beaubourg, looking north. The first left is Impasse Beaubourg. Note the oval sign, the same as in the photo above.

▼ Same spot today. Rue Beaubourg with Impasse Beaubourg on the right.

▲ 43 to 57 Rue Beaubourg, looking north, circa 1900. This is only about 20 meters farther along the street than the previous photo.

▶ Same view today. The first building dates from 1905 and the second building from 1903.

Rue Michel-le-Comte ➐

▲ The Cabaret du Bon Puits at the corner of 52 Rue Beaubourg (cross street) and 36 Rue Michel-le-Comte (in the foreground). Note the sign on the left corner of this building (Vidal) and match it to the building on the extreme left in the top photo on the next page. (photo, Pottier, 1901)

▶ Same view today. (photo, Dot Barad)

▲ The men on the right are standing in front of 52 Rue Beaubourg, at the corner of Rue Michel-le-Comte. Note the sign on the extreme left of the photo (Vidal) and match it to the building on the extreme left in the top photo on the previous page.

▼ Same view today. Rue Beaubourg. On the left, Rue Michel-le-Comte.

▼ Rue Beaubourg, east side of the street. The arrow indicates number 52, seen in the photo above. (photo, Atget)

Rue du Grenier-Saint-Lazare ⑧

▲ The corner of Rue Beaubourg, right, and on the left, Rue du Grenier-Saint-Lazare. In the foreground, going off to the right, is Rue Michel-le-Comte. The building under the arrow still stands.

▶ Same view today. The corner building dates from 1923.

Rue Beaubourg ❾

Formerly Rue Transnonain, the section of Rue Beaubourg between Rue Michel-le-Comte and Rue au Maire was opened in the early 17th century. It ran alongside a Carmelite convent, torn down at the Revolution. The street was renamed Rue Beaubourg in 1851.

▶ Rue Beaubourg, looking north. The first right is Rue Montmorency. The second building with the awnings, 62 Rue Beaubourg, was formerly a theater, the Doyen. It is visible on pp. 158, bottom left, and 159, top, as well. (photo, Atget; Musée Carnavalet, June 1901)

▼ Same view today.

◀ In blue, Rue Beaubourg. Outlined in red, the Carmelite convent with the cemetery of Saint-Nicolas. (map, Delagrive, 1744)

▶ Rue Beaubourg looking north. The building on the right is 62 Rue Beaubourg, visible on the previous and next pages pages in the top photos. The red line indicates a store awaiting demolition, that of a Mr. Zimmerman, also visible in the photo below. The building on the left with the green line is on the corner of Rue Chapon.

▲ Same view today.

▼ 62 Rue Beaubourg. The store with the red line is the same as in the photo above. (photo, Pottier, 1913)

▼ Same view today. The building on the extreme left is the same in the photo above.

▲ Rue Beaubourg, looking south. The building in the middle, number 62, formerly the Doyen theater, is visible on the two previous pages. Just after this building is the corner of Rue Montmorency. (photo, Atget, 1901)

▲ In the foreground, a new and wide Rue Beaubourg stops at Rue Chapon. On the right sit the remains of a building recently demolished. The red lines show how narrow the street had been. Note the buildings between the blue lines, demolished and replaced by a more modern structure in the photo below. (photo, Pottier, 1914)

◄ Same view today.

▲ Rue Beaubourg, looking south from Rue au Maire. (photo, Marville)

▼ Same view today. The building on the right is the same in both photos.

▲ View of Place des Victoires with Rue Etienne-Marcel on the right. (postcard, circa 1900, private collection)

▼ Map showing projected path of Rue Etienne-Marcel, in red, cutting through the old neighborhood to Rue Montorgueil.

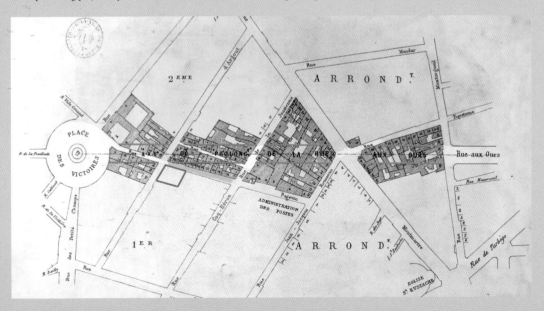

Rue Etienne-Marcel

Haussmann's grand design for the Right Bank included a continuous thoroughfare from Place des Victoires through the Marais to Boulevard Beaumarchais. This plan was only carried out as far as Rue Beaubourg with the cutting through of Rue Etienne Marcel and the widening of Rue aux Ours and Rue du Grenier-Saint-Lazare under the Third Republique. Only partial work was carried out for the completion of the new street beyond Rue Beaubourg, which explains anomalies such as the widening of Rue Michel-le-Comte at Rue Beaubourg, why Rues des Quatre-Fils and de la Perle suddenly widen, and why the building at the corner of Rue Roger Verlomme and Rue des Tour-nelles is so strangely situated.

▲ Corner of Rue Etienne-Marcel and Rue de la Hérold. The building on the right is a vestige of old Rue Pagevin, brown and green on the map.

Rue du Grenier-Saint-Lazare ➊
Rue Michel-le-Comte ➋

▲ Rue du Grenier-Saint-Lazare looking west from Rue Beaubourg. The houses on the right side predate the street widening.

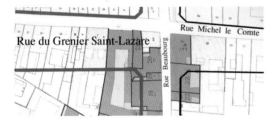

▲ A narrow Rue Michel-le-Comte looking east from Rue du Grenier-Saint-Lazare. The buildings on the left and right show the projected width of the new street that was to be cut through following Haussmann's plan for the continuation of Rue Etienne-Marcel.

◄ The planned extension of Rue du Grenier-Saint-Lazare through Rue Michel-le-Comte. Only the blue portion was carried out.

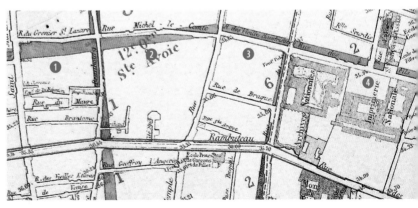

▶ Rue Etienne-Marcel in its projected length cutting through the Marais. (1878)

Rue des Haudriettes ③
Rue des Quatre-Fils ④

◀ Same view today. The fountain on the corner dates from around 1705 and was moved back when the buildings on either side were demolished.

▲ Rue des Haudriettes on the right, and Rue des Archives on the left.

▶ Rue des Quatre-Fils, looking west. In 1935 portions of the buildings on the right were demolished and their facades moved back in order to allow for a wider street to be cut through in front. The street was never finished, and today all that remains is a uselessly wide sidewalk. A poor trade.

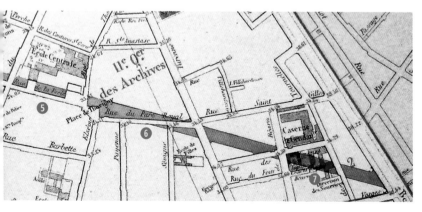

Rue
de la Perle ❺

▶ Rue de la Perle. The building with the peaked roof is number 22. These buildings were demolished in 1914 for the anticipated extension of Rue Etienne-Marcel. The arrow points to a building still standing. (photo, Pottier, August 1905)

▼ Same view today.

◀◀ (top left) 24 Rue de la Perle. (photos, Lansiaux, 1916)

◀◀ (top right) 6 Rue de la Perle. Demolished. (photo, Lansiaux, 1920)

▶▶ 20 Rue des Quatre-Fils. Demolished. (photo, Pottier, 1914)

Rue du Parc-Royal ⑥

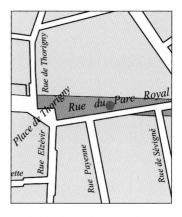

▲ The blue dot marks 12 Rue du Parc-Royal.

▲▼ Rue du Parc-Royal. All these buildings were slated for demolition for the extension of Rue Etienne-Marcel.

▲ The staircase of the Hotel de Croisilles, completed in 1620, at 12 Rue du Parc-Royal. It would have been lost in the extension of Rue Etienne-Marcel.

Rue Roger Verlomme ⑦

▶ The sign on top shows Haussmann's wish to extend Rue Etienne-Marcel this far.

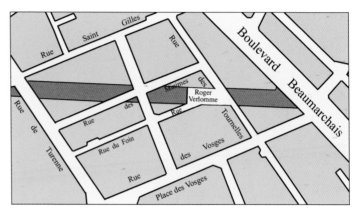

▲ Proposed new Haussmann street cutting through the Marais as part of a continuous thoroughfare from Place des Victoires to Boulevard Beaumarchais.

▲ Rue Roger Verlomme from Rue des Tournelles. The building on the right, which dates from 1912, is oddly placed in relation to the street because it was to be the beginning of Haussmann's continuation of Rue Etienne-Marcel to Boulevard Beaumarchais.

▲ Avenue de l'Opéra. (postcard, circa 1900)

Avenue de l'Opéra

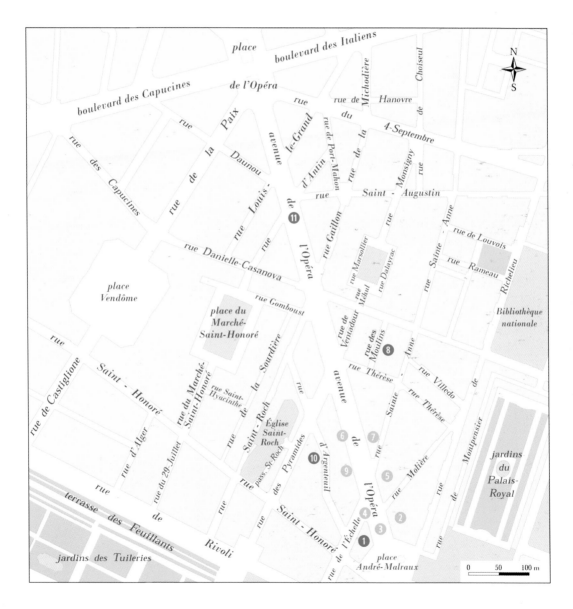

Avenue de l'Opéra ❶

Avenue de l'Opéra was conceived by Baron Haussmann in 1854 and inaugurated by General MacMahon in 1877. The idea for the avenue was twofold—to clean up the area around the Louvre and Tuileries and to create a thoroughfare linking the Rue de Rivoli to the boulevards and to Gare Saint-Lazare. The two ends of the avenue were built first, from Place André-Malraux to Rue de l'Echelle in 1854 and from Rue Louis-le-Grand to Boulevard des Capucines in 1864. The middle section was completed in 1878, a year after the avenue's inauguration on January 7, 1877. The idea of placing the opera house on the boulevard was not proposed until 1860.

La Butte des Moulins

The Porte Saint-Honoré of the Charles V fortification stood at about the place of today's Rue Saint-Honoré and Rue de Richelieu. Just to the north at about the site of today's Avenue de l'Opéra and Rue des Pyramides was a hill, Butte des Moulins (see the brown circle on the map). Created in the 14th century using earth and gravel from the construction of the Charles V wall, the butte was also an execution site. Common thieves were hung, forgers were burnt at the stake, and counterfeiters were boiled alive in water or oil. It was from this hill in 1429 that Joan of Arc launched her assault on Paris in a failed attempt to free the city occupied by the English.

The hill was partially leveled and built upon in the 17th century and totally razed in 1875. The earth from the hill was used to level the Champs de Mars.

▲ Avenue de l'Opéra in construction. In the distance, la Butte des Moulins is being leveled. Haussmann planted trees on the avenue, but Charles Garnier argued for an unobstructed view of his new opera house and prevailed, thus creating the only avenue in Paris without trees. The sidewalk and building on the left are new construction and are visible in the present-day photo. (photo, Marville)

▼ Same view today. The first street on the left is Rue de l'Echelle.

▲ Avenue de l'Opéra looking south from Rue de l'Echelle towards Place André-Malraux. In the foreground sits a mound of rubble from demolished houses. (photo, Emonts, January 1877)

◀ Same view today.

Opening of Avenue de l'Opéra

The new avenue, in light green, erased one of the most historic quarters of old Paris, a network of narrow streets between Rue Saint-Honoré at the bottom and Rue des Petits-Champs at the top: Impasse de la Brasserie* in red near the bottom and Passage Saint-Guillaume* in green next to it, two passages that stood very near to today's Place André-Malraux; Rue de l'Anglade* in purple to their left; the intersection of Rues des Orties*, des Moulins*, l'Evêque*, and des Moineaux* in red; and Rue du Clos-Georgeau* in blue.

▲ Avenue de l'Opera under construction. (photo, Marville)

▼ The red shading marks the approximate location of Passage Saint-Guillaume* and Impasse de la Brasserie*. Compare to the following pages.

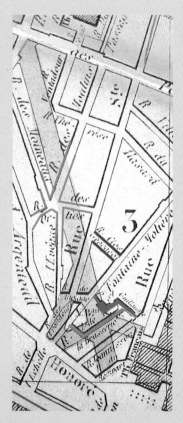

Passage Saint-Guillaume* ❷

▼ Passage Saint-Guillaume*, constructed in 1780, exiting onto Rue de Richelieu. To the right is Impasse de la Brasserie*. The map on the previous page shows Passage Saint-Guillaume* in dark green. (photo, Marville, 1864)

Impasse de la Brasserie* ❸

► Impasse de la Brasserie* looking south from Passage Saint-Guillaume*. (photo, Marville, 1865)

◄ Rue de la Fontaine-Molière, looking north, also the site of today's Rue Molière. On the right, Impasse de la Brasserie*was demolished for Avenue de l'Opera. (photo, Marville)

Rue de l'Anglade* ④

▲ Rue de l'Anglade* towards Rue l'Evêque*
from Rue Fontaine-Molière. The first right is
Rue Sainte-Anne. (photo, Marville, 1866)

▼ Same view today. In
red, the approximate
location of Rue de
l'Anglade*. In blue, Rue de
la Fontaine-Molière.

Rue du Clos-Georgeau*❺

▲ Rue du Clos-Georgeau* from Rue Sainte-Anne. (photo, Marville)

▼ Same view today. The red lines indicates where Rue du Clos-Georgeau* began from Rue Sainte-Anne.

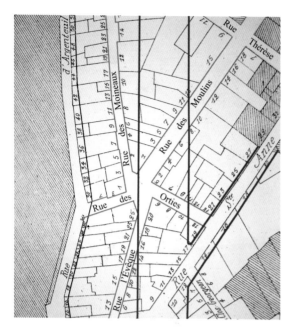

Intersection of Rues des Orties*, des Moulins*, des Moineaux*, and l'Evêque* ❻

▲ Intersection of Rues des Moulins*, des Moineaux*, des Orties*, and l'Evêque*. These streets were obliterated by Avenue de l'Opéra, in blue.

► Rue des Moineaux*. On the right, Rue des Moulins*. Note the water fountain on the right. The corner building is also visible at the end of the street on p. 180 (the building with the arch), and on p. 182. (photo, Marville, 1865)

Rue des Orties*

▶ Rue des Orties* from Rue Sainte-Anne towards Rues des Moineaux* and des Moulins*. Note the arch at the end of the street on Rue des Moineaux* and compare to the next page. (photo, Marville, 1864)

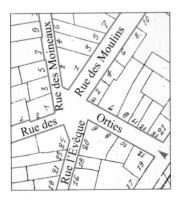

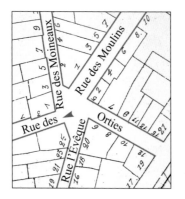

▼ Rue des Orties* looking west towards Rue d'Argenteuil. On the left, Rue l'Evêque*. On the right, Rue des Moineaux*. (photo, Marville, 1864)

Rue des Moulins* ⑧

▲ Rue des Moulins* looking towards Rue des Petits-Champs. On the left, Rue des Moineaux*. On the right, Rue des Orties*. The building on the left corner is also visible on p. 179. Note the water fountain with buckets waiting to be filled. (photo, Marville)

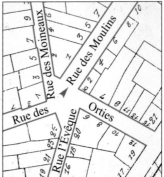

Rue l'Evêque*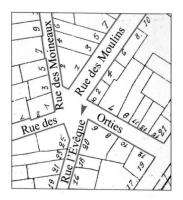

▼ Rue l'Evêque* looking
south from Rue des Orties*
towards Rue des Frondeurs.
(photo, Marville, 1865)

Rue d'Argenteuil ⑩

▼ Rue d'Argenteuil looking north. The celebrated French dramatist, Pierre Corneille, lived in this street at number 18 and died there in 1684. (photo, Marville, 1864)

Rue Saint-Augustin and Rue d'Antin ⓫

▲ Avenue de l'Opera from Rue Saint-Augustin, right, and Rue d'Antin, left. (photo, Marville, 1877)

◄ Same view today.

▲ Rue de la Grande Truanderie. This section of the street was demolished for the creation of Rue Turbigo. (photo, Atget, 1907)

Les Halles

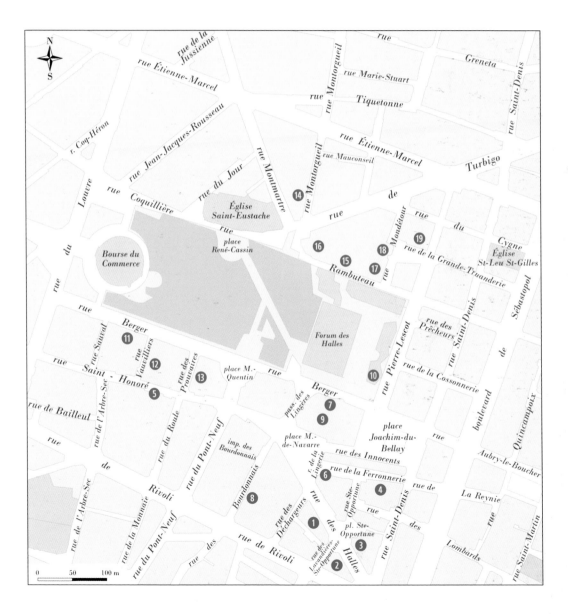

The Baltard Pavilions in Les Halles

The story of Les Halles is well known and almost too sad to recount. Its demolition and subsequent rebuilding in the 1970s has been universally recognized as a catastrophe of urban planning. To read accounts of the hopes and aspirations of the renovation from the urban planners and to see the result is heartbreaking. An operation on this scale in a quarter so deeply tied to Parisian history, indeed the Parisian psyche, required the skill and care of a surgeon picking up a scalpel. Unfortunately it was the mind of a bulldozer.

Few people argued against moving the market out of Paris. The congestion created by the hundreds of trucks rolling daily into Paris created a stranglehold on the city. But what to do with Baltard's pavilions? London was faced with the same problem but chose to keep the structure of the market, Covent Garden. Today it stands as a thriving destination point for Londoners and tourists alike.

Parisians protested the loss of the pavilions, but it was too little too late. One person appalled at the prospect of losing this gem of 19th-century French architecture was American Orrin Hein. Dining in Les Halles at Au Pied du Cochon in September 1970, he remarked to a Parisian friend on the beauty of these giant structures. "Have a good look," his friend said. "They won't be here much longer. They're going to be torn down."

► ► The belly of Paris has been gutted. In the distance on the left is the 16th-century Church of Saint-Eustache on Rue Rambuteau, created in 1836 by Prefect Rambuteau. Most of the buildings seen here will also be torn down in this massive redevelopment project.

▼ Les Halles early in the morning.

399. PARIS — Un coin des Halles le matin   G. M.

▲ Orrin Hein, the American who wanted to buy the Baltard pavilions and transport them to the United States. (1971)

◄ May 25, 1971. Young people protesting the loss of Les Halles in a pavilion converted into a skating rink. The placards read, "No to the closing of Les Halles."

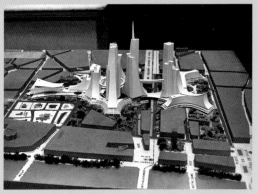

▲ Alicia and Hieronim Listowski's project for the makeover of Les Halles, seen from the Bourse du Commerce. (1971)

▲ Model of a redone Les Halles conceived by architect Jean Faugeron in the 1960s.

▼ The Forum des Halles, replacing the old central market, inaugurated September 4, 1979. Thirty years later, the decision was made to tear it down and start over.

Hein contacted Marcel Diebolt, the prefect of the Seine, and told him he wanted to purchase the Baltard pavilions and transport them to America. Probably not taking him seriously, Diebolt telegrammed back, "The pavilions are yours free; all you have to do is pay for their dismantling and transport. Four million dollars," the prefect said, probably thinking this sum would discourage a purchase. Hein returned to America and formed the US Committee for the Preservation of Les Halles.

Several weeks later, Hein contacted Diebolt from New York, intending to close the deal. Instead, Diebolt did an about-face. Dismantling the Baltard pavilions was impossible, he said. "Too much breakage and too late." Dubbed "Superman" by

the Parisian press, Hein appealed directly to President Georges Pompidou, who wanted to be known as a great protector of French cultural heritage. The loss of these pavilions would be a taint on his legacy, Hein stated. Several days later, a communiqué from the president's office announced that one of the pavilions would be saved. Today it stands in the suburb of Nogent-sur-Marne.

Not long after Bertrand Delanoe was elected mayor of Paris in 2001, he began a project for the demolition and rebuilding of Les Halles. From the thirty architects who entered the first stage of the competition, four finalists were chosen to present models for a new vision of Les Halles. They included Winy Mass and Rem Koolhaas from Holland,

and Jean Nouvel and David Mangin, both French. Mangin carried the day. To date no work has been undertaken on the site.

Unfortunately, the modern buildings on the south side of Rue Berger and the north side of Rue Rambuteau will remain in place because they are owned privately rather than by the city.

▼ The future Les Halles, designed by Patrick Roger and Jacques Anziutti, to be carried out by the firm of Seura-Mangin. The model for the competition was constructed by Alain Hugon with the help of Thierry Martin. (photo, Arnaud Rinuccini)

Rue des Halles ❶

◀ The creation of Rue des Halles in 1854, in red, eliminated Rue des Fourreurs*, in blue.

▼ Rue des Fourreurs* looking north.

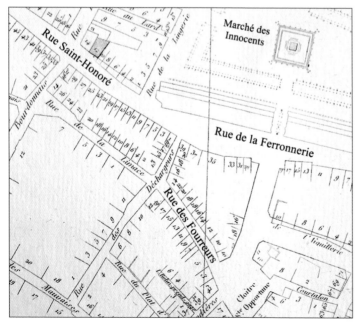

▲ Rue des Halles looking northwest towards Les Halles.

◄ Les Halles before the creation of Rue des Halles. This network of streets was seriously rearranged in two stages, first when Rue des Halles was created, and second when the Baltard pavilions were torn down in the 1970s.

Paris. — La Rue des Halles

Edit. M. S., Paris.

▲ Rue des Halles looking towards the central market Les Halles. The building on the right with the red line stands on Place Sainte-Opportune and was demolished.

► Same view today. On the right, Place Sainte-Opportune.

Rue des Lavandières-Sainte-Opportune ❷

▼ Same view. See the first building on the left in the photo above.

▲ Rue des Lavandières-Sainte-Opportune from Rue de Rivoli. The buildings to the right of the red line were demolished for the creation of Rue des Halles. (photo, Marville)

Place Sainte-Opportune ❸

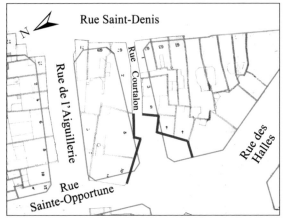

▲ Place Sainte-Opportune. Directly to the right of the narrow street is the Bureau des Lingères, built in 1716, but gone today. See the next page.

◄ Red lines indicate Haussmann's plans for redoing this area and the obliteration of Place Sainte-Opportune. The *place* was opened on the site of the ancient Cloister of the Church of Sainte-Opportune (9th century), which was confiscated during the Revolution and demolished in 1797. Haussmann's plan was only partly achieved. The widening of Rue Courtalon and Rue de l'Aiguillerie was never carried out. Place Sainte-Opportune, outlined in blue, was saved.

▲ Place Sainte-Opportune.

▶ The Facade of Bureau des Lingères was first moved to Square des Innocents in 1902. Note the Baltard pavilion through the arch. (photo, Seeberger)

▼ The same facade was moved again and installed on the facade of 22 Rue Quincampoix.

Rue de la Ferronnerie ➍

▲ Rue de la Ferronnerie towards Rue des Halles and Rue Saint-Honoré. The first right is Rue de la Lingerie.

◀ Same view today. Note that the Haussmann building with an awning on Rue de la Lingerie is gone.

▼ Same view today.

▲ Rue de la Ferronnerie looking east from Rue Saint-Honoré before Rue des Halles was created. On the left, Rue de la Lingerie. Henri IV was assassinated in front of 11 Rue de la Ferronnerie on May 14, 1610, when his carriage was blocked in traffic. (photo, Marville)

Rue Saint-Honoré ⑤

▶ Rue Saint-Honoré from Rue des Déchargeurs, looking west. On the right, Rue de la Lingerie. Everything between the red lines stands today and is the same in both photos. Everything else was demolished. (photo, Marville)

◀ Same view today.

Rue de la Lingerie ❻

▼ Same view today. (photo, Dot Barad)

▲ Rue de la Lingerie, late 1960s. The building with the red line at the corner of Rue des Innocents still stands. The Haussmann building to the left, although in perfect condition, was torn down as part of the unfortunate redevelopment of Les Halles. The other end of this building is visible in the photo, bottom right, on p. 202. (photo, Roland Liot)

▲ Rue de la Lingerie looking towards Rue Saint-Honoré. This street dates from the 12th century. Its name derives from the women whom King Saint-Louis authorized to sell their linen and clothing goods here in the 13th century. On the right, Rue de la Poterie*. Compare to the photo on the next page. The buildings on this street were torn down and replaced by Haussmann, and in turn were torn down during the 1970s renovation of Les Halles. They in turn were torn down for the buildings that stand in contemporary Paris. (photo, Marville)

Rue de la Poterie* ❼

▲ Rue de la Poterie* looking west from Rue de la Lingerie. (photo, Marville)

◀◀ Facing page, bottom left. Rue de la Lingerie in demolition. The Baltard pavilions are new, and Rue Berger has just been opened. The building on the left with the rounded roof is visible in the Marville photo above.

◀◀ Facing page, bottom right. Rue de la Lingerie north in the 1960s. The only structure standing today is the Métro entrance. All the rest was demolished in the 1970s. (photo, Roland Liot)

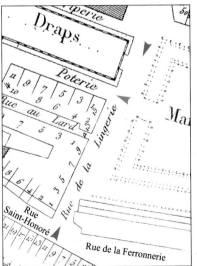

◀ The red arrow indicates the point of view of the Marville photo on the previous page; the blue arrow, the point of view of the photo on this page; and the green arrow, the point of view of the bottom right photo on the previous page.

Rue des Bourdonnais ⑧

▲ Rue des Bourdonnais (Rue Lenoir in the map on the next page) south towards Rue Saint-Honoré. On the left, Rue au Lard*. On the right, Impasse au Lard*. Match the street lamp and the sign on the left, indicated in red, to the photo on the next page. The building with the green line on its facade is on Rue Saint-Honoré. It still stands and is visible on p. 200 (the first building after the red line). Everything else has been demolished. (photo, Marville)

Rue
au Lard* ❾

▼ The red arrow indicates the point of view of the photo of Rue des Bourdonnais (Rue Lenoir) on the facing page. Compare the blue arrow to the contemporary photo on the right.

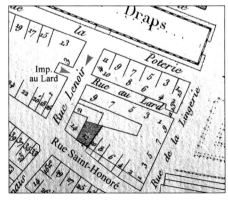

▲ Rue au Lard* from Impasse au Lard* across Rue des Bourdonnais. Beyond the arch lies Rue de la Lingerie. Compare the red sign and lamp to the photo on the previous page. (photo, Marville)

▶ Same view today after redevelopment in the 1970s.

Rue Pierre-Lescot ⑩

▲ Rue Pierre-Lescot looking north. The first street on the left is Rue Berger. Compare the chimney to the same on the next page. Everything on the left has been demolished.

▶ Same view today.

Rue Berger ⑪

▲ Rue Berger looking west. The first street on the right is Rue Pierre Lescot. The Baltard pavilion pictured here is the same one in the photo on the preceding page. The first three buildings on the right still stand.

◄ Same view today.

▲ Rue Berger looking west. On the left, Rue de la Lingerie. Everything except the buildings in the far distance has been demolished.

◀ Same view today.

▲ Rue Berger looking west towards Rue du Louvre. (photo, Barry)

▶ Same view today.

Rue Vauvilliers ⑫

▼ Same view today. The red building on the left is also in the bottom photo on the next page. The first building on the right is of recent construction.

▲ Rue Vauvilliers, looking south. On the left and right, Rue des Deux Ecus (present-day Rue Berger). Compare the lamp colored blue to the same at the top of the Marville photo on p. 212. Everything to the right of the red line was demolished in 1907. (photo, Marville)

◀ Rue Vauvilliers seen from Rue Berger. The building with the blue lamp on the preceding page has been demolished.

▼ Corner of Rue Vauvilliers (right) and Rue Berger (left) around 1960.

▶ Rue Vauvilliers looking north towards Rue du Jour. The first left is Rue des Ecus. Compare the blue lamp to the one in the top photo on p. 210. (photo, Marville)

▼ Same view today.

▶▶ Les Halles before the demolition of the Baltard pavilions in 1971.

Rue des Prouvaires ⑬

◀ Rue des Prouvaires, looking north with the Baltard pavilion at the end of the street. (photo, Marville)

▼ Same view today. With Les Halles gone, the Church of Saint-Eustache closes the view today.

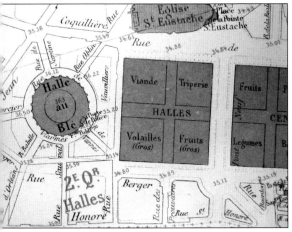

Rue Montorgueil ⑭

◀ Rue Montorgueil before the creation of Rue Turbigo. The red line indicates buildings still standing.

▼ Same view. In the foreground, Rue Turbigo.

▼ Rue Turbigo (in red) opened in 1858 to faciliate traffic around Les Halles. The arrow indicates the point of view of the photos on this page.

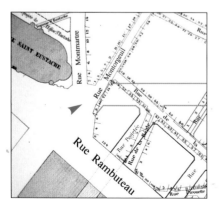

Rue Rambuteau ⑮

2310 Paris — Carrefour des Rues Turbigo et de Rambuteau (1ᵉʳ et IIᵉ arrᵗˢ)

F. F.
Paris

▲ On the extreme left, the Church of Saint-Eustache. Rue Turbigo is on the left. On the right, Rue Rambuteau. All the buildings in the center were demolished in the 1970s. The Métro entrance is no longer there. (postcard, circa 1900, private collection)

◄ Same view today.

▲ Rue Rambuteau looking west. This street was constructed between 1834 and 1838 as a link between Les Halles and the Marais. The building with the red line still stands; see the contemporary photo below. In the distance, Church of Saint-Eustache. (postcard, circa 1900, private collection)

▼ Same view today. Only the first three buildings on the right survived the Les Halles makeover.

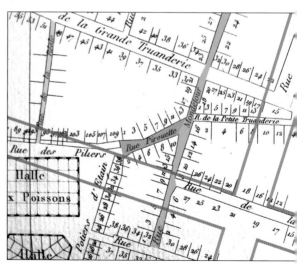

Rue de la Réale* ⑯

◀ Rue de la Réale* from Rue Rambuteau around 1860. (photo, Marville)

▼ Same view today.

◀◀ The creation of Rue Rambuteau (in red) separated Rue Pirouette* (in blue) from Rue des Piliers*. It also shortened Rue Mondétour (in green). A new building was constructed in the triangle formed by Rues Rambuteau, Mondétour, and Pirouette* but was demolished in 1911. Gray lines indicate Rue Pierre-Lescot. In orange, Rue de la Réale.

Rue
Pirouette*⑰

▲ Rue Pirouette* from Rue Rambuteau.

◄ Same view today.

Rue Mondétour ⑱

◄ Rue Mondétour from Rue Rambuteau. The building on the right is the same in the contemporary photo and is lined in red on p. 216.

▲ Same view today.

Rue de la Grande-Truanderie ⑲

551. - PARIS. - La Rue de la Grande Truanderie. - *G. I.*

▲ Rue de la Grande-Truanderie from Rue Pierre-Lescot. Rue Mondétour runs along the buildings on the left. The red line corresponds to the building on the next page.

▶ Same view today. Compare the buildings on the right to the photo above.

▲ Hotel at the corner of Rue Mondétour and Rue de la Grande-Truanderie. (photo, UPF)

Epilogue

As I have studied the transformation of Paris, one question comes to mind. What will Paris look like one hundred years from today? This is the question that seizes my mind again and again.

Personally, I am worried. My fear is that one day people entering Paris by automobile will pass signs on the street with arrows directing them to "Centre Historique." This is what I call the "Paris of the Postcards" central Paris, where all the tourists roam, the 1st through the 7th arrondissements. This Paris will remain largely intact, as will the 8th and 16th, if for no other reason than they are wealthy neighborhoods.

However, I fear that the rest of Paris, the outer arrondissements beyond the center that the tourist never sees, will become a solid wall of nondescript high-rises no more interesting than what we see today en route to Paris from the airport. Already, massive redevelopment in these quarters shows us that the edge of Paris is a permeable boundary where the dreariness of the suburbs creeps into the city, suffocating entire neighborhoods with gargantuan, faceless, boring boxes. In the 20th arrondissement, we have Nouvelle Belleville; in the 19th, the Orgues de Flandre; and in the 15th, the Front de Seine: masses of bureaucratic concrete and steel spawning ennui and alienation in a landscape of "no-there-ness." Most deplorable, many of these structures are made of materials that age poorly. In place of the patina of the historic buildings of Paris, we see decrepitude. Even Haussmann did better.

While it is unlikely that central Paris will undergo massive public-works projects à la Haussmann, it is still not sufficiently protected. The risk today is that it will die the "death of a thousand cuts," nothing massive, only small "renovations" here and there. The building at 35 Rue Mazarine in the 6th arrondissement is an example. It was torn down around 1997. The new building is similar in scale and design to the building it replaces but lacks a ground-floor shop. One door leads to apartments upstairs, with another, larger door for underground parking. The facade of the building stands mute, as if a small section of the street had been anesthetized, eliminating any interaction with the public. The older, adjacent buildings all have shops at ground level that create liveliness and demonstrate why Paris is one of the world's great walking cities.

Whom can we depend on to see that Paris is not served up as a sacrifice to the beast of progress in the decades to come? We would like to trust our civic leaders, but their decisions don't always warrant that trust.

After the success of Pompidou's unfortunate expressway along the Right Bank of the Seine, the Voie Express Rive Droite, plans were put in motion for the same thing on the Left Bank. But in another example of Paris urbanism determined by accident, Pompidou's sudden death in 1974 brought his plans to a halt. The newly elected President Valéry Giscard d'Estaing, with preservation in mind, cancelled the project.

Jacques Chirac was appalled by this development and in 1977 stated:

> Abandoning the project for the Voie Express Rive Gauche was one of the biggest mistakes of our time. Those responsible for this decision will be viewed by history as demagogues and incompetents. This is an immense project that Paris should undertake with vigor and enthusiasm. I am ready to restart the operation. It will happen one day. It is written in the future of Paris.

In one respect, the pendulum has swung back the other way. Today Mayor Bertrand Delanoe has undertaken a major program to rescue the city from the automobile and make Paris more pedestrian-friendly. Sidewalks have been widened, and parking has been eliminated (on Rues de Buci, Danton, and Francois-Miron). The number of automobile lanes on major streets has been reduced, and more bike lanes have been installed. Yet this same mayor plans to undertake major building projects on the periphery of the city to create satellite communities that will dwarf Paris proper in scale. The danger is that over time, they will continue being built until they encircle the city and then will encroach on the city itself.

The pendulum swings. How will it swing in the decades to come?

It is my wish, not as a native Parisian, of course, but as someone who has adopted Paris as the city that lies at the center of my heart and mind, that my grandchildren's children, and their children again, will have the opportunity to know Paris as I have known it: not as a city rendered dead through commodification, efficiency, and a brutal notion of progress, but rather as a city whose beauty will inspire them as it has inspired me and millions of others, and whose values exalt the full richness and subtlety of human experience.

Photo Credits

All contemporary photographs of Paris are by Leonard Pitt unless otherwise noted.